OBSESSION

MEANS DE MATERIAL

AUDIENCE

DISUADED FASHION

WE REQUIRE YOU TO LEAVE IN A

RDERLY

MANY OF THESE IMAGES WERE OBTAINED THROUGH NETWORKS OF ASSOCIATED COLLABORATORS. WHEREVER POSSIBLE WE HAVE SOUGHT TO ATTRIBUTE, INVOLVE AND CREDIT [BLAME?] THE SOURCE. THESE CREDITS ARE LISTED TOWARDS THE BACK OF THE BOOK, ALONG WITH DECLARATIONS OF OBSESSIONS, MEANS, MATERIALS AND AUDIENCE BY OUR VARIOUS CONTRIBUTORS. A RELATED WEBSITE DEVELOPS THE PROJECT FURTHER AND INVITES YOUR PARTICIPATION.

WWW.WHEREISHERE.COM

IMPOUNDED AT

55

COMMON

WHERE

LAURENCE KING

HE BORDERS OF

HW ICATION: ISHERE

IDEAS MATERIALS IMAGES NARRATIVE TOXINS

LEWIS BLACKWELL, P. SCOTT MAKELA +
LAURIE HAYCOCK MAKELA

PAULA CARSON, ASSISTANT EDITOR

PUBLISHED 1998 BY LAURENCE KING PUBLISHING   AN IMPRINT OF CALMANN & KING LTD
71 GREAT RUSSELL STREET LONDON WC1B 3BN

A CATALOGUE RECORD FOR THIS BOOK IS AVAILABLE FROM THE BRITISH LIBRARY. ISBN 1 85669 141 1
PRINTED IN ITALY

DESIGNED BY P. SCOTT MAKELA + LAURIE HAYCOCK MAKELA WITH WARREN CORBITT. ADDITIONAL ASSISTANCE BY KURT MILLER

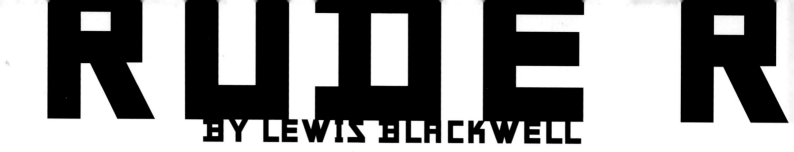

RUDE R

BY LEWIS BLACKWELL

HOW DO YOU LIKE TO RELATE TO YOUR AUDIENCE?
BY INVITATION
ENGAGEMENT
SEDUCTION
THROUGH PROPOSITION
ASSAULT
POSSESSION
OTHER [PLEASE SPECIFY]

FINE. BUT JUST ONE SMALL POINT: WHO ARE YOU TO THINK YOU MIGHT HAVE AN AUDIENCE? IN THIS CENTURY WE HAVE BEEN TOLD BY SOME LEADING THINKERS THAT WE HAVE AN UNAVOIDABLE DIALOGUE WITH THE AUDIENCE. AND THE NATURE OF A DIALOGUE IMPLIES THAT THE AUDIENCE IS RECIPROCATING, SENDING SIGNALS BACK; IT IS IN AN UNAVOIDABLE DIALOGUE WITH THE PERFORMER. EACH PERFORMS FOR THE OTHER. SUCH A RELATIONSHIP, IN ANOTHER CONTEXT, COULD BE PRESENTED AS A FETISH, AN EXCHANGE OF SELF-GRATIFICATION.

Which leads to the alternative take on this: that there is no dialogue, but rather monologues. We don't really exchange. Instead we are trapped within behavioural patterns. The media is more significant than the mediators. It is the all-encompassing thing that we statically surround, taking our significance from it, rather than it being created by us. Consider Darwin's theory of evolution taken into media theory, with all its inevitability of interaction and change, and you have a sense of how insignificant the notion of a "creative act" is in such a vision.

In this analysis, any idea of being a "creator"—through images, words or other projected experiences—is illusory. This is somewhat ironic: if you thought you were concerned with the illusions created by attempts to communicate, now you end up being presented with the illusion of such an action in the first place. You are left with only a sense of self to deconstruct as you melt down into a philosophized, psychoanalyzed messy blob. You and your putative audience [and its sense of you] is just part of a system so much larger, with dimensions impossible to conceive.

EMARKS

This gives one interpretation of the complexity and contradiction [qv.] of much late 20th century production. As the creative operatives [designers, writers, architects, directors and so forth] are increasingly doubtful of any meaningful direction to their work [beyond its power to involve and entertain themselves in a sense of performance], so they forego being responsible for trying to effect change in their audience. Instead, they are simply struggling to assert their own existence. Trying to get a grip on

WHEREISHERE.

The practical challenge: how to get a clear voice to be heard in the mass-hysteria of mass-media.

THE FIRST OBSTACLE: TO CLEAR YOUR VOICE.

INDEED,

TO HAVE A VOICE.

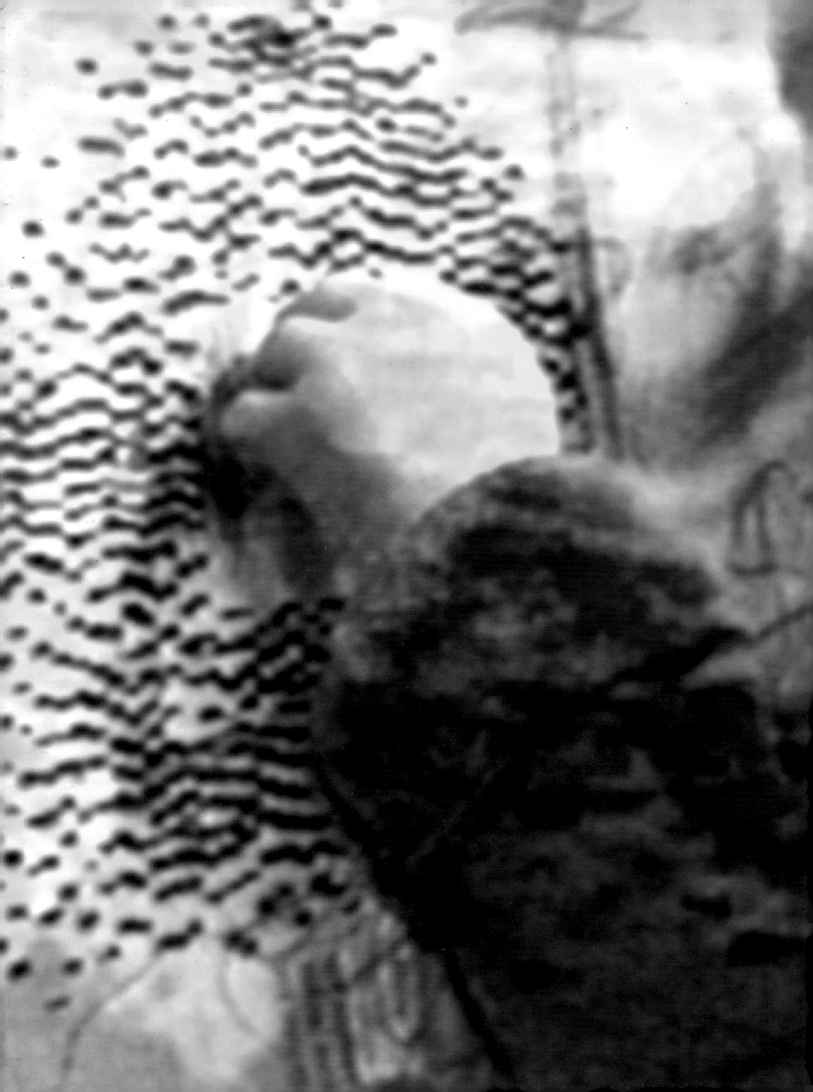

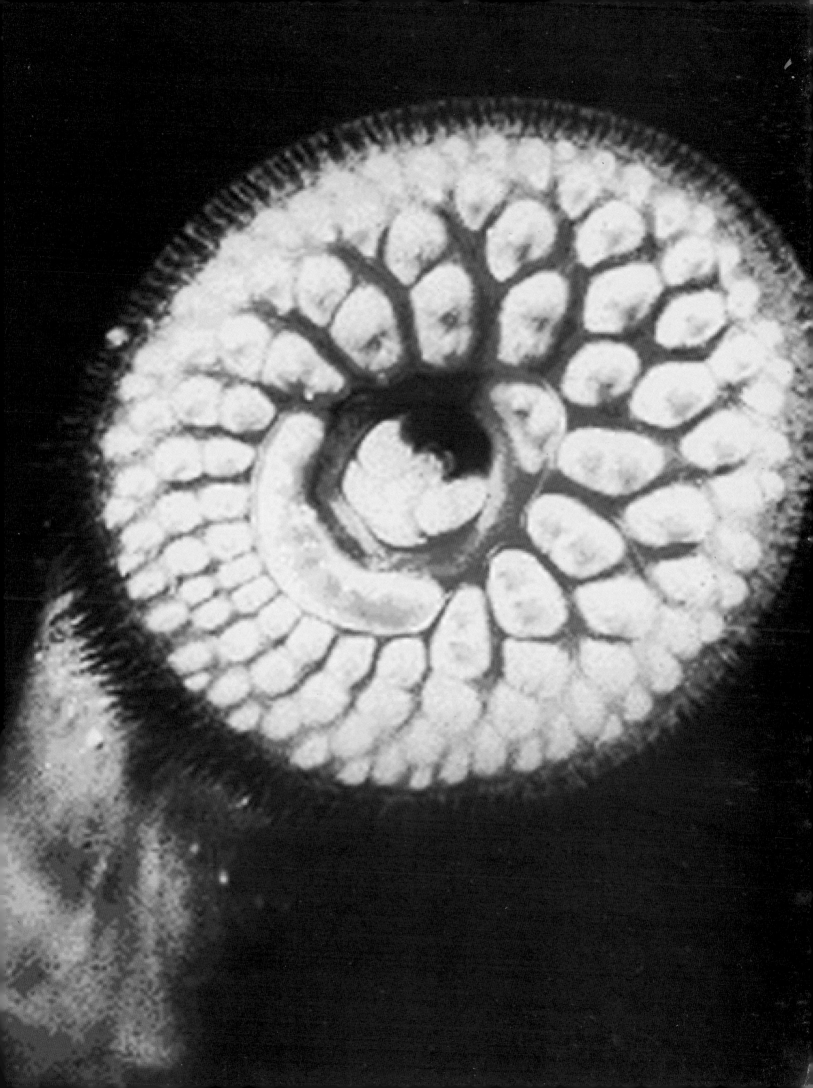

MEANSM
MANIPU

BY LEWIS BLACKWELL

THE MEANS ARE THE INTERMEDIARIES. THEY ARE THE MEDIA. THEY ARE VERY CLEVER IN THAT THEY ALWAYS JUSTIFY THE ENDS. NEVER ASSUME THE MEANS ARE WITHOUT THEIR OWN AGENDA.

YOU MAY CHOOSE YOUR MEANS, BUT THE MEANS ALSO CHOOSE WHAT YOU DO WITH THEM. SUB-ORGANISMS THEY MAY BE, YET THEY HAVE A LIFE AND THEY FIGHT TO PRESERVE IT. THEY KNOW HOW YOU WANT TO BE. THEY ARE AHEAD OF YOU AND COLLECTIVELY THEY DESCRIBE HOW OTHERS WILL SEE WHAT YOU WANT TO BE. YOU ARE NEVER VISIBLE WITHOUT THEM.

CONSIDER HOW SIMPLE MEANS SHAPE THE WAY WE WORK. DO YOU EAT WITH A PENCIL? DO YOU COOK WITH A CAMERA? THE MEANS INFLUENCE METHOD, AND HABITS OF METHOD STEER US TOWARDS CERTAIN MEANS. THE ECONOMICS OF COLLECTIVE HABIT, I.E. MASS-MEDIA, FORCE US DOWN A ROUTE OF BEING OBLIGED TO USE THE SAME MEANS AGAIN AND AGAIN.

As the media becomes us, we become its willing slaves. The extreme of this is summarized in the position of the French philosopher Jean Baudrillard who has taken up photography in recent years . . . or rather, photography has taken him up. He says the pictures take themselves, suggesting the moment and the frame. He is a mere auxiliary. His pictures are exhibited, published. They look cool. They look cutting-edge professional.

As means give form to us, so materials give form to means.

The materials are the tools. They are useful. Like the means they can also manipulate the manipulator. But while the means are transparent, the materials are almost always lumpenly visible. They signal their presence . . . indeed, that's about all they do without assistance.

That's where we come in. We recognize materials need help to do something else with themselves, and we help them. This is not a kind gesture. It is one motivated by immense greed as we covet the earth.

Two anti-heroes of American culture nailed it down a century or so ago: "The ideas of the class which is the ruling material force of society, is at the same time its ruling intellectual force". This suggests that if you are in control of the materials, you are in pole position to determine the intellectual area. Rupert Murdoch may not have read Karl Marx and Friedrich Engels of late, but he is certainly living out their vision.

Even if you are not a global media mogul on first-name terms with only the top presidents and prime ministers, you will signal your existence through media [means] and substance [materials]. You will shape, you will be shaped. Designers, photographers, art directors, directors, illustrators, typographers, editors and many others, do this as proxy voters signalling for corporations, institutions, brands, causes and more.

Every now and then they stop playing at what they think they should be on somebody else's behalf, and try to do it for themselves. Sometimes they have nothing of themselves to recognize, nothing to work with through means and materials. Burnt-out cases, but a condition that can often free up their work. Sometimes they have lots to release, but struggle to find the means, to afford the materials.

And, finally, here before we pause, an in memoriam wrapped as a question for us: are words means or materials? In other words, media or tools? We could say they are both, as are so many means and materials.

In which case what can we make of dead words—those many excised from this text, for instance, highlighted and deleted, thrown into the void—do dead words cease to mediate? Can they be means and then no longer, but always exist as materials? But do deleted words still exist in a black hole of edits? Are they just mediating in a different way, memories of what used to be?

Now memory . . . the means, the materials, the hidden manipulator, coloured by obsession. Let the memories speak true.

ADDITIONAL NOTES

The publisher would like you to read something that is useful, easily digested, ordered in such a way that it can be a practical guide to the contents of this book. A "how to" do this at home. Something along the lines of those handy essays that sit at the front of an annual. A few well-chosen words that summarize the summary that follows. He really wants it in this book, but as these contents present themselves most truly as themselves, and the other texts are best read using the words contained therein, we can bring you the bonus of a commentary on another book and exhibition.

In 1997 London's Royal Academy mounted one of its most successful exhibitions, "Sensation". This contained work loaned from the modern art collection of Charles Saatchi, a trawl of recent years that included many of the most provocative pieces of art from modern British artists. The images, objects, artists and their lost intentions are for elsewhere. But to help you in your work, here are some of the highlights of the materials demonstrated at the show. This is an approved and proven list for success in creating art. Should you stray from this canon it would be as well to seek advice. Finally, some tips on what's going to be big next year:

SILICONEMAPMAPPINSPAPERALUMINIUMTIGERSHARKFORMALDEHYDETENT MATTRESSMDFWASHBASINANDFITTINGSCANVASWOODGESSOGLASSMAGGOTS SUGARSTEELPOLYESTERRESINFIBREGLASSVELVETBLOODELEPHANT'S DUNGROPEOILPAINTHOUSEHOLDPAINTC-TYPE COLOURPRINTSPLASTERRUBBERMIRROREDACRYLIC

The oil exuded from the heads of goats [best embedded in fragrant pearl encapsulation technology for a standout print finish].

PAPERBAGSRATS.

LOVE
IS A HEMORRHAGE
BY LAURIE HAYCOCK MAKELA

THREE MONTHS AFTER A BRAIN HEMORRHAGE, I SAT ON A BEACH IN JAMAICA, ABLE TO PINPOINT EXACTLY THE PHYSICAL SENSATIONS WITHIN MY CRANIUM, PRESSURES OF DENSE MATTER PACKED AGAINST SHELVES OF BONE. I COULD FEEL THE WEIGHT OF ITS PARTS, SOME PULSING MORE THAN OTHERS. I TURNED MY HEAD SLOWLY THOSE DAYS, CRADLING THE TENDER SEGMENTS OF THE CONTAINER OF MY INTELLIGENCE.

THE HEMORRHAGE FOLLOWED THREE SEQUENTIAL ORGASMS IN THE LADIES ROOM OF A TRENDY RESTAURANT IN SOHO, NEW YORK. THAT MOMENT OF EXTREME PLEASURE SET OFF A CONGENITAL TIME BOMB: A MALFORMATION OF A TINY BLOOD VESSEL EXPLODED INTO A POOL OF BLOOD IN THE LEFT FRONT HEMISPHERE OF MY BRAIN. INSTANTLY, A MASSIVE HEADACHE TOOK HOLD FOR ABOUT SIX WEEKS, SLOWLY DIMINISHING UNTIL JAMAICA, WHERE I REALIZED THAT THE EGGSHAPED SPACE IN MY HEAD THAT FILLED WITH BLOOD WILL ALWAYS BE A ZONE OF INSTABILITY. BLOOD VESSELS ALWAYS SLIGHTLY AGITATING THE CORAL-LIKE HOUSE OF BRAIN.

THE EXPANSE OF JAMAICAN SKY AND OCEAN ONLY MADE THE THICKENED ZONE IN MY HEAD MORE ASSERTIVE: I COULD ACTUALLY FEEL THE <u>THINGNESS OF THINKING</u>.

AGRAPHIA Four days after the hemorrhage I sat in a wheelchair in front of 50 or so neurology students at Cornell University in New York while a famous neurologist lectured his students on my case. The intern presented information about my admissions and treatment, with particular attention to my youth [40] and my occupation [graphic design]. The bleed had affected the part of the brain that makes meaning out of symbols—I had a form of aphasia which created a partial loss of the ability to write and read. My ability to read was levelled to that of my 6 year old daughter. The famous neurologist demanded the students answer this: "what is the most important fact of this case?" After six tries from six students he bellowed "she is here!" **THE BRAIN DOES NOT FEEL** My dad died unexpectedly the same year as Elvis, 1977. But instead of overdosing in Gracie Mansion, he had a heart attack in his office building's toilet. My brother died the same year, city, and style as Kurt Cobain, both suicides as instant as a bullet to the head. Unlike Elvis and Cobain, they didn't die because of the pressure of being famous, they died because of the disappointments of being average. Survival, therefore, is to become something special. **PRE-LITERACY** The summer following the hemorrhage I visited my brother—a Zen monk—in Seoul, Korea. I learned something about wordless teaching and the demonstrative argument. The Zen master uses a technique called the koan to sharpen the mind. "What is this?" he might ask the student, holding up one finger. With the speed and precision of dueling swords, the student answers "this". "Where is here?" he asks, looking the student in the eye. The student answers here

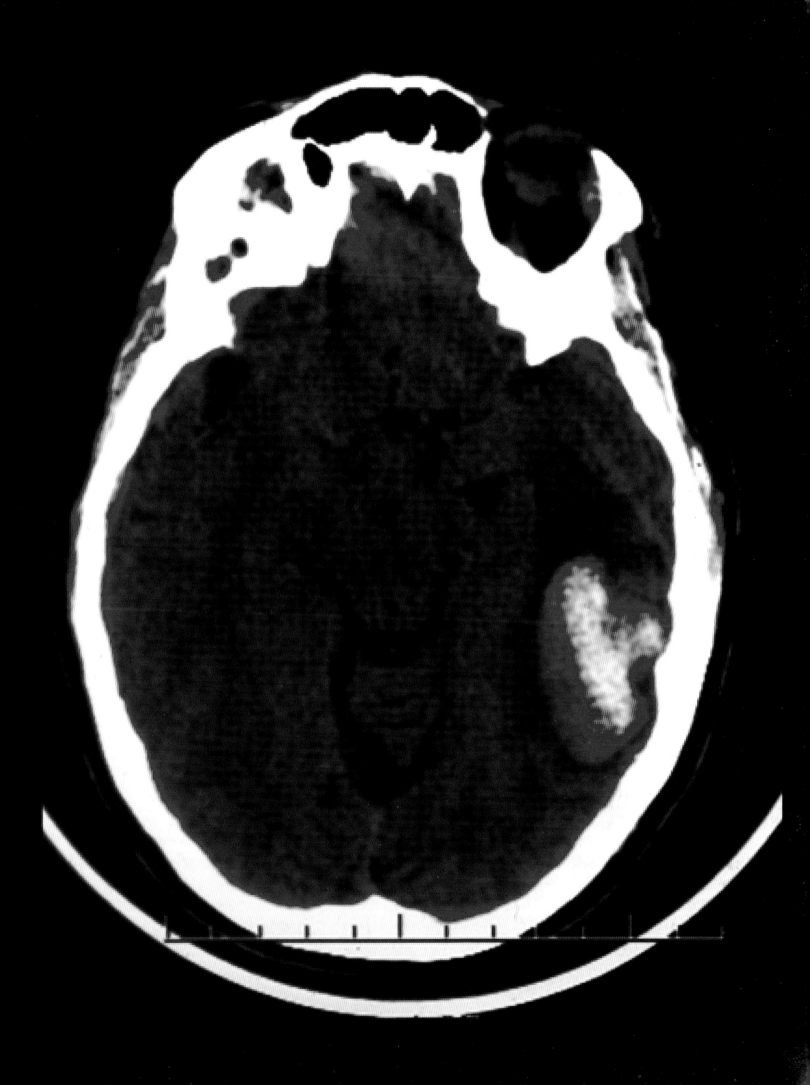

NOITISOP
THE

OBSESSION
IS YOUR

IGNITION, SWAG, FOOD AND PAYLOAD. YOU, THE DOG WITH
ITS TEETH URGENTLY IN A BONE, DIGGING FOR YOUR PERSONAL
CENTER OF AROUSAL AND GRATITUDE—CRITICAL AND ANTI-CRITICAL,
WIDE AWAKE AND HUNGRY, ADDICTED AND MEDITATIVE.

AUDIENCE
IS REAL.

SELECT YOUR NETWORK,
TRANSMIT AND BE WIDE OPEN TO RECEIVE.

MEANS
ARE THE TOOLS

DELIVERING YOUR OBSESSION STREAM.

DE-MATERIAL
SURFACES

BREAK OUT OF FRAMES OF PAPER AND CATHODE. IF THERE ARE
ATOMS PRESENT THERE IS A SURFACE. MEANING CAN EXIST ABOVE,
BELOW AND BEYOND THE ASPECT RATIOS WE KNOW TOO WELL.

POSITION
IS A MAPPING

A SINGLE-POINTED HOLD ON A PHALANX OF RIVERS + TERRITORIES
OF THE SUPER-RETINAL. I AM THE PIMP, WHO KNOWS HOW TO SELL
TRUTH AND FANTASY. VISUAL SEDUCTION IS SHINY,
TIGHT AND DIRECT.

RESPOND
TO THE NIPPLE THAT FEEDS
THE CURRENT CONDITION
THE STATE OF BEING
THE PRESENT MOMENT

OBSESSION

MEANS   DE MATERIAL

AUDIENCE

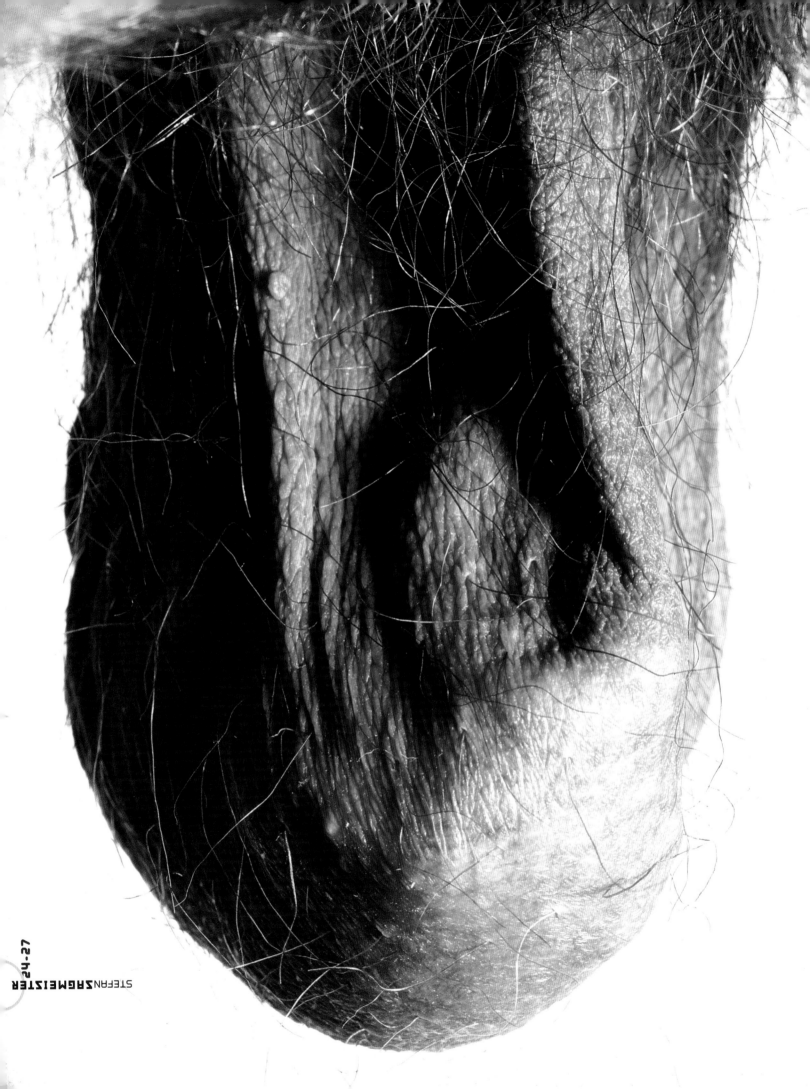

WHERE IS HERE

ART vs DESIGN

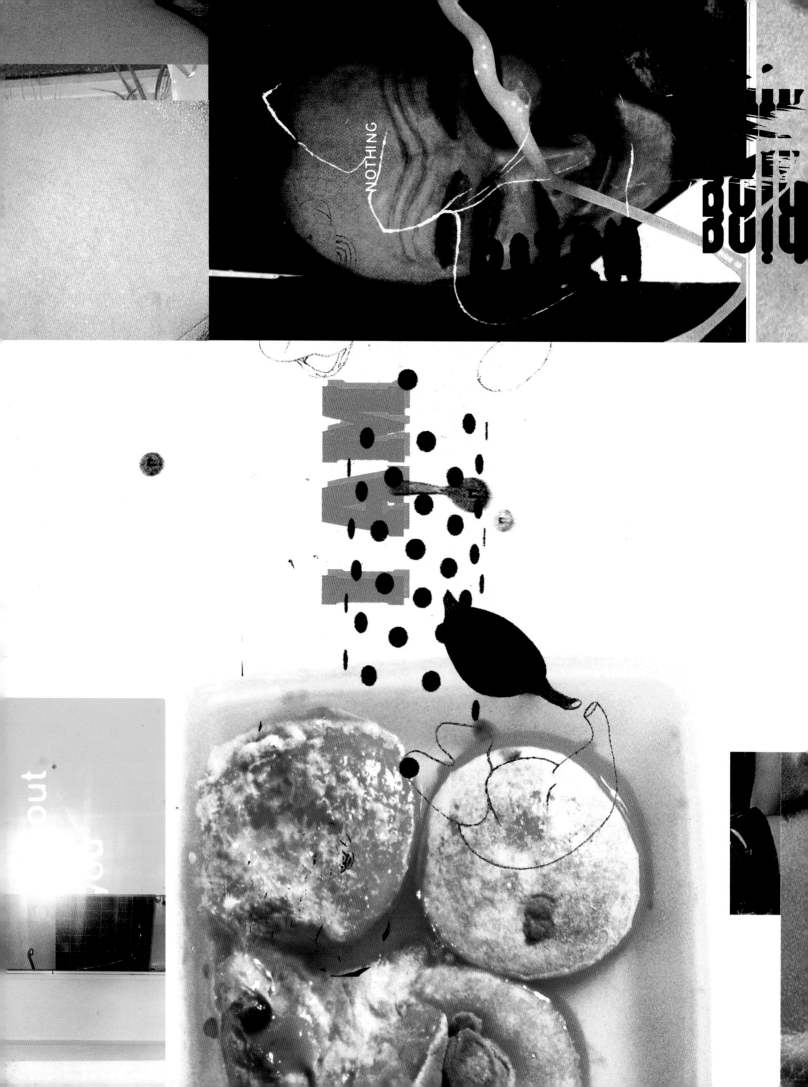

Zone Books
Distributed by The MIT Press
FEHLP ISBN 0-942299-41-8

FANTASIES TAKE THE FAMILIAR AND MAKE STRANGE

OTHER
SOMETHING
AROUND
IT
TWIZTING

The blurring
of our
boundaries
suggests
the shape of
new terrain.

Rice School of Architecture

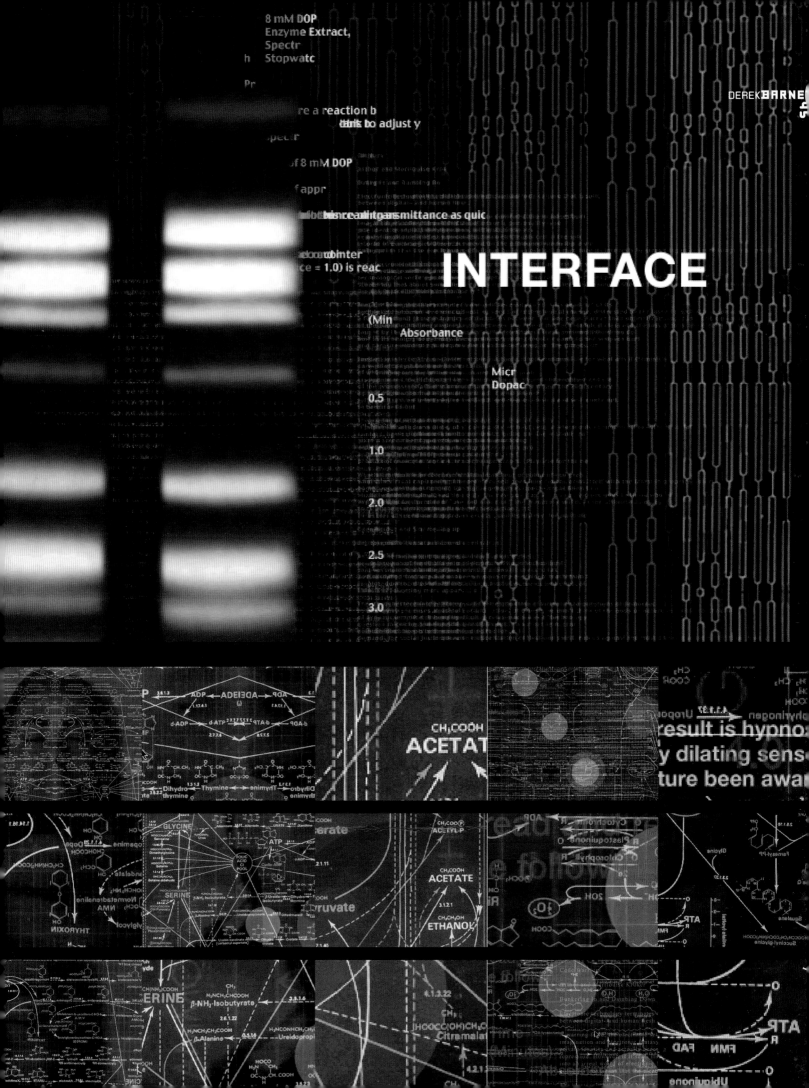

abcd7

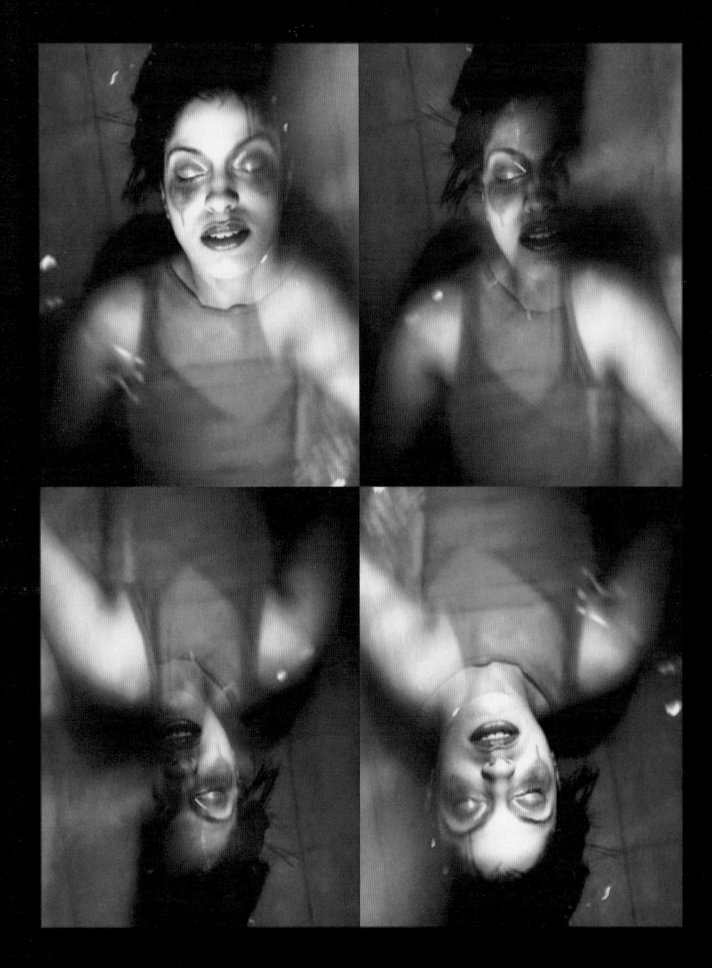

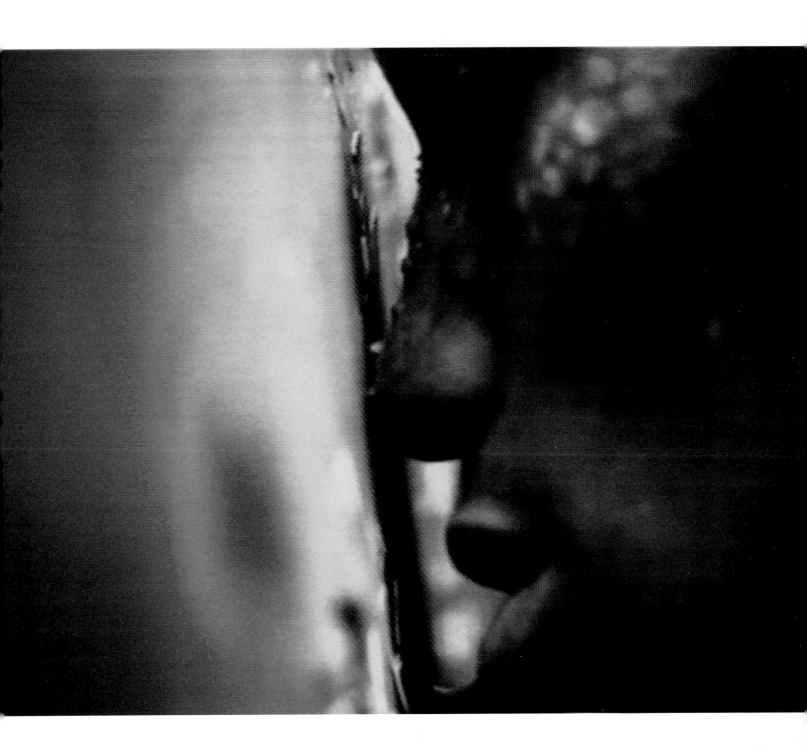

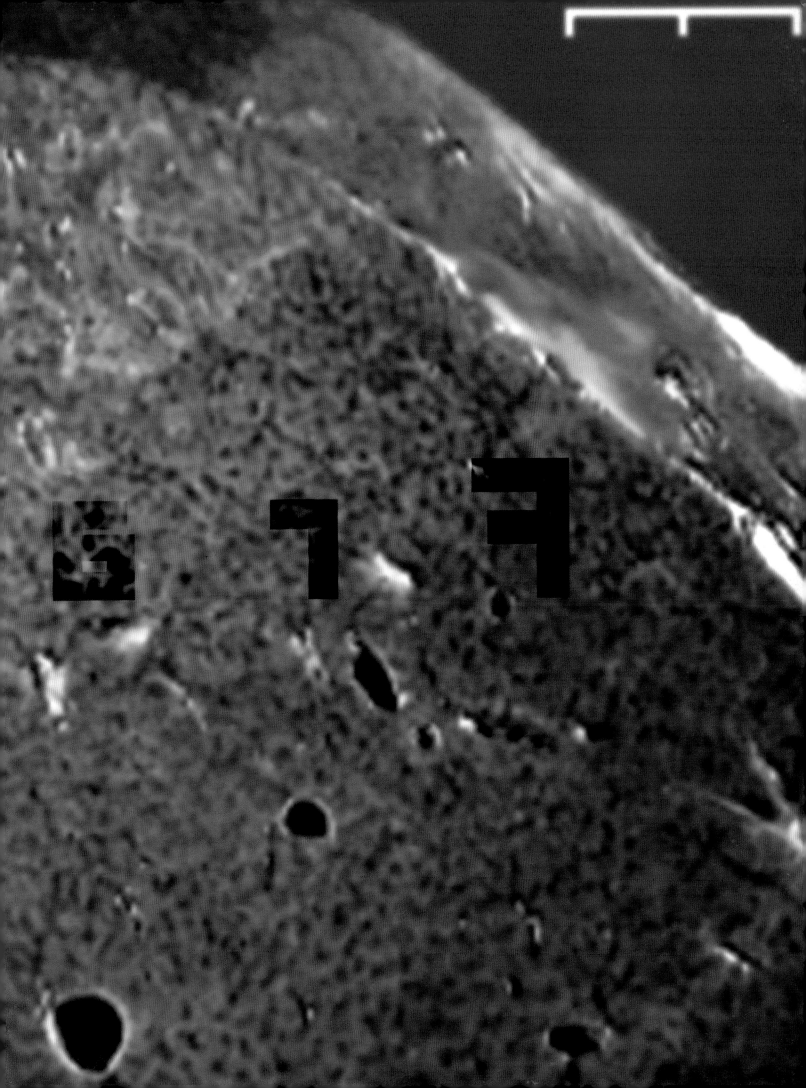

choose your amnesia

a case	a time			
	1 month	1 year	10 years	3 days
Gulf war				
collaboration				
Algeria				

I made my choice. Did you?

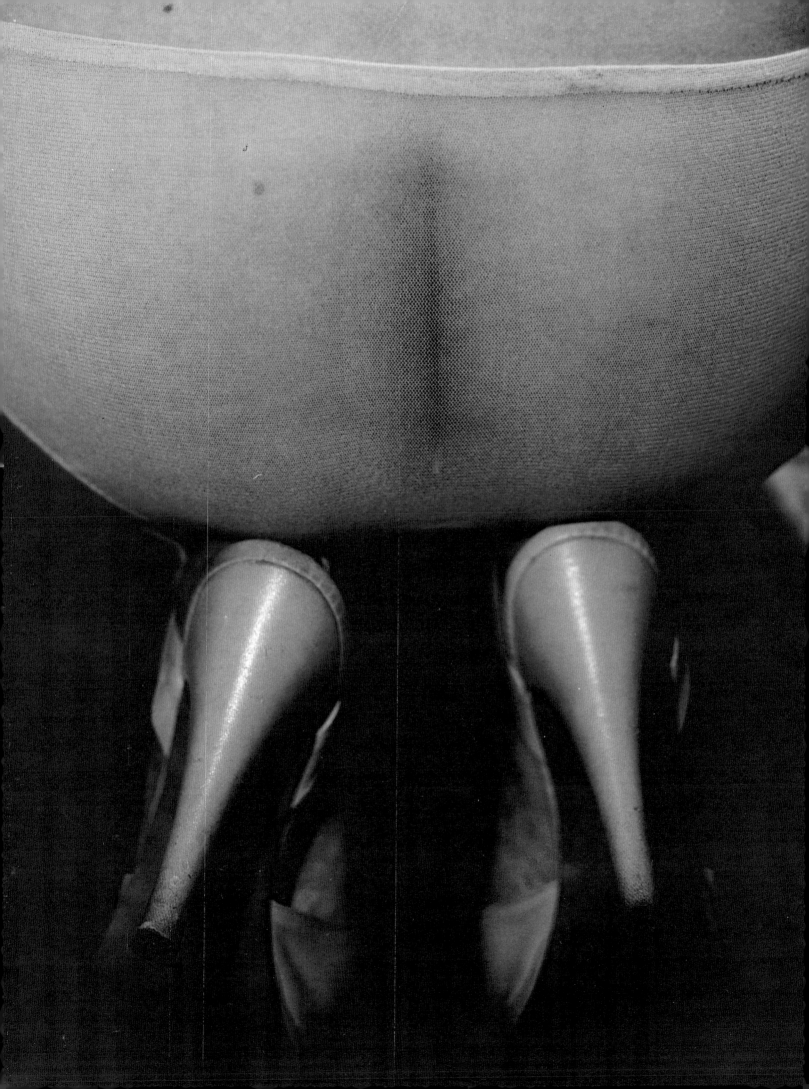

we oo o no

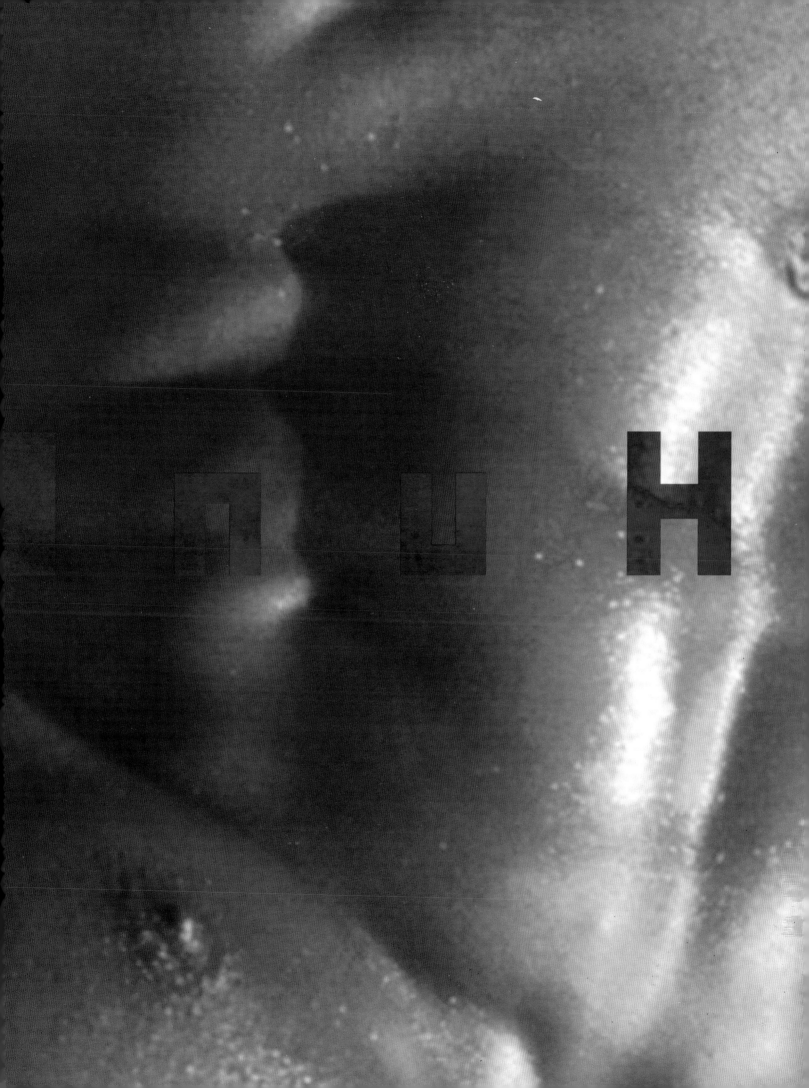

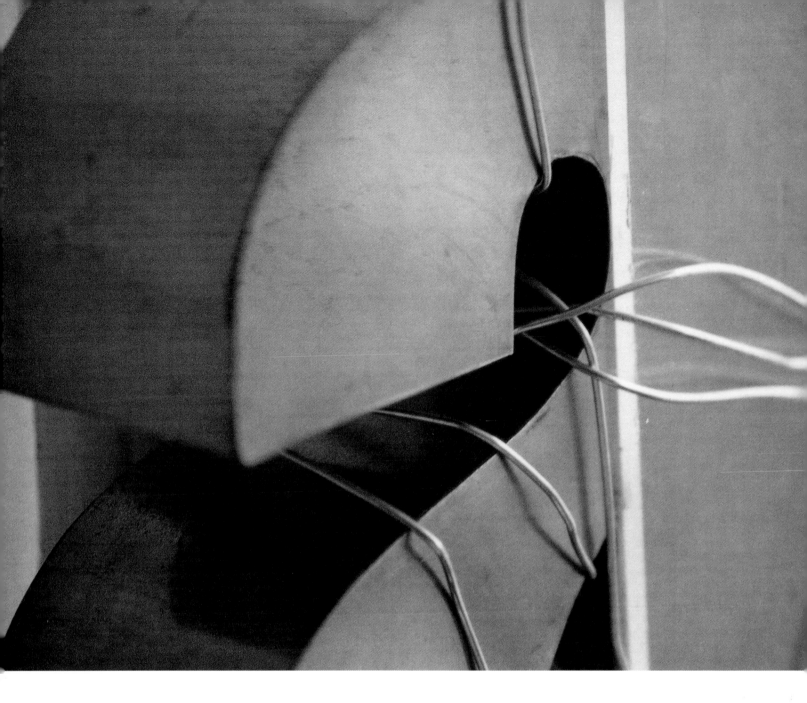

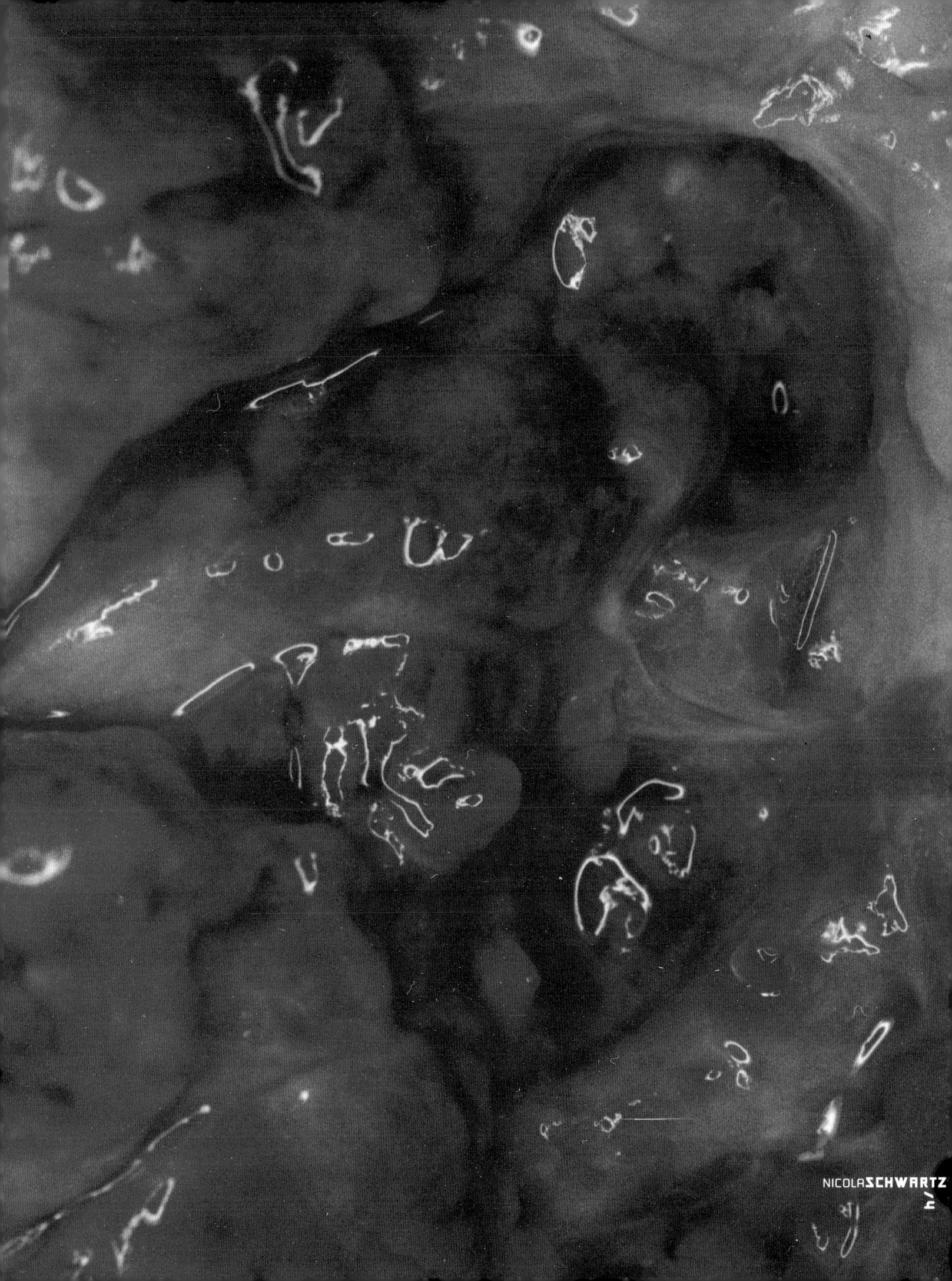

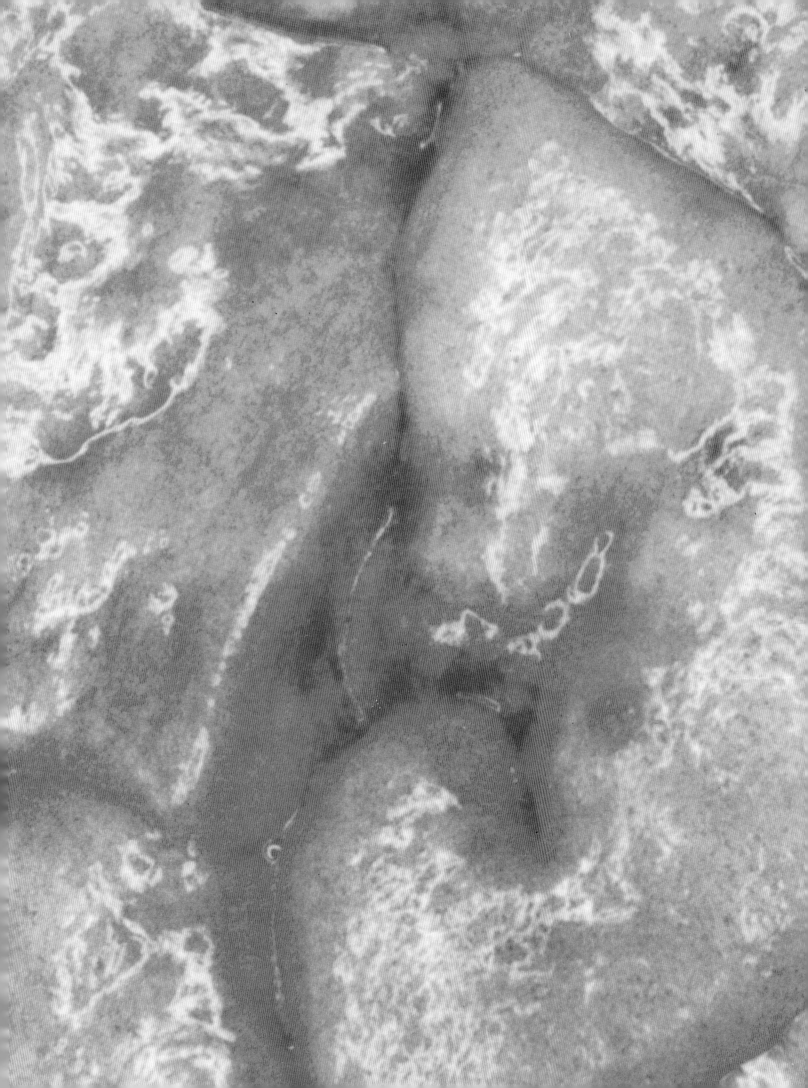

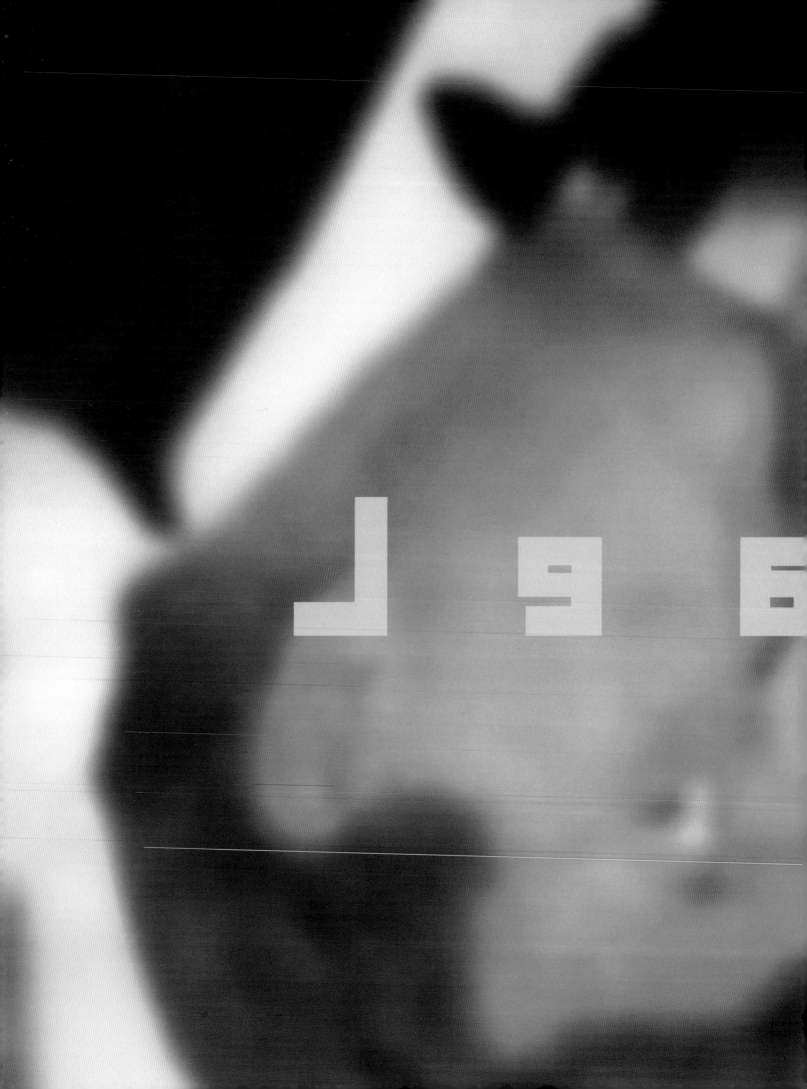

1Z1

HIRO **SUGIYAMA**
&

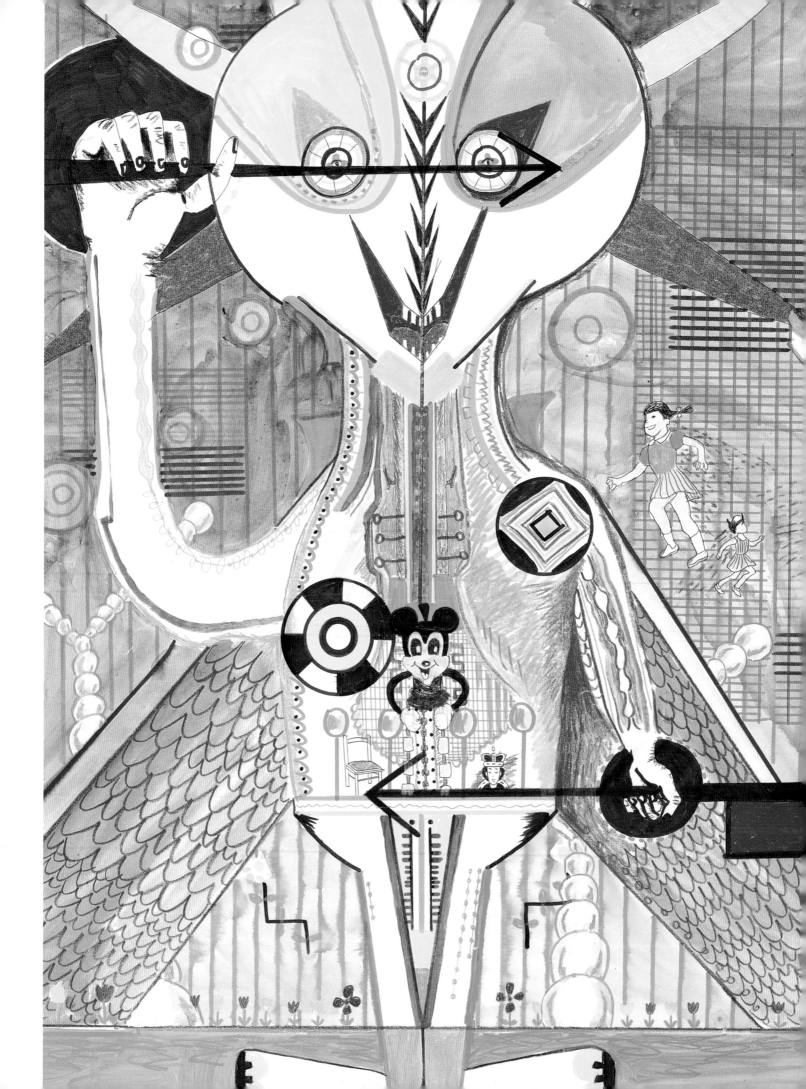

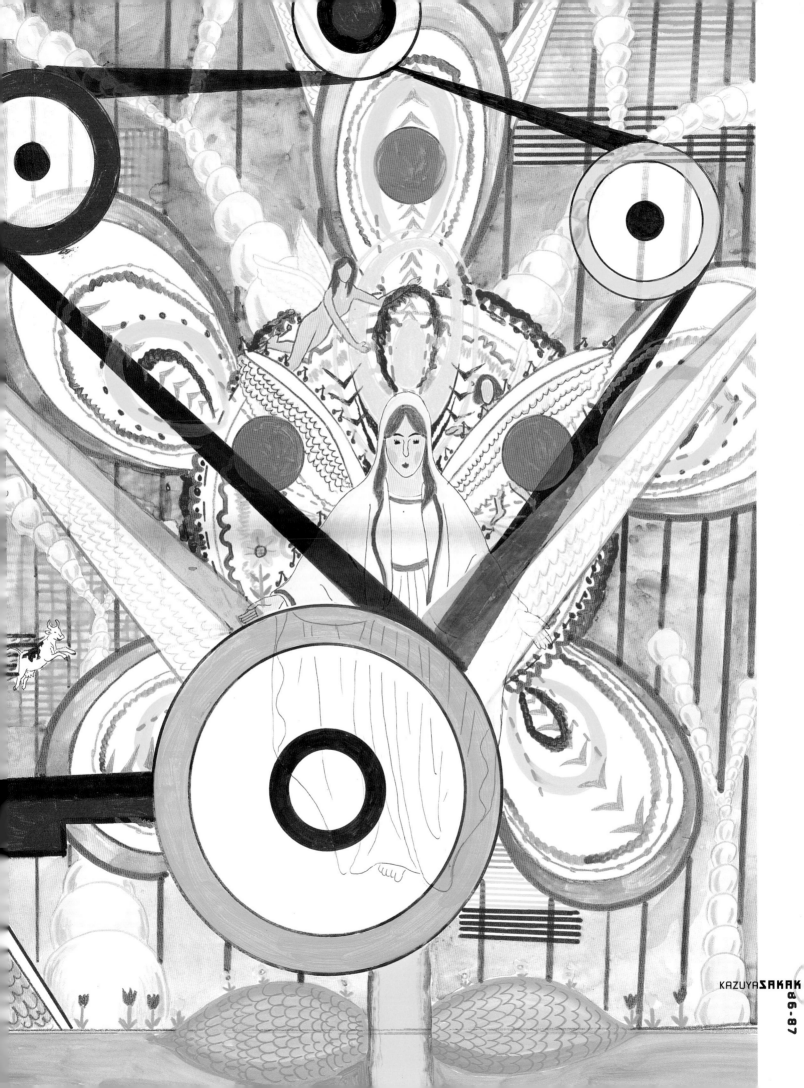

KAZUYA**SAKAK**

86·87

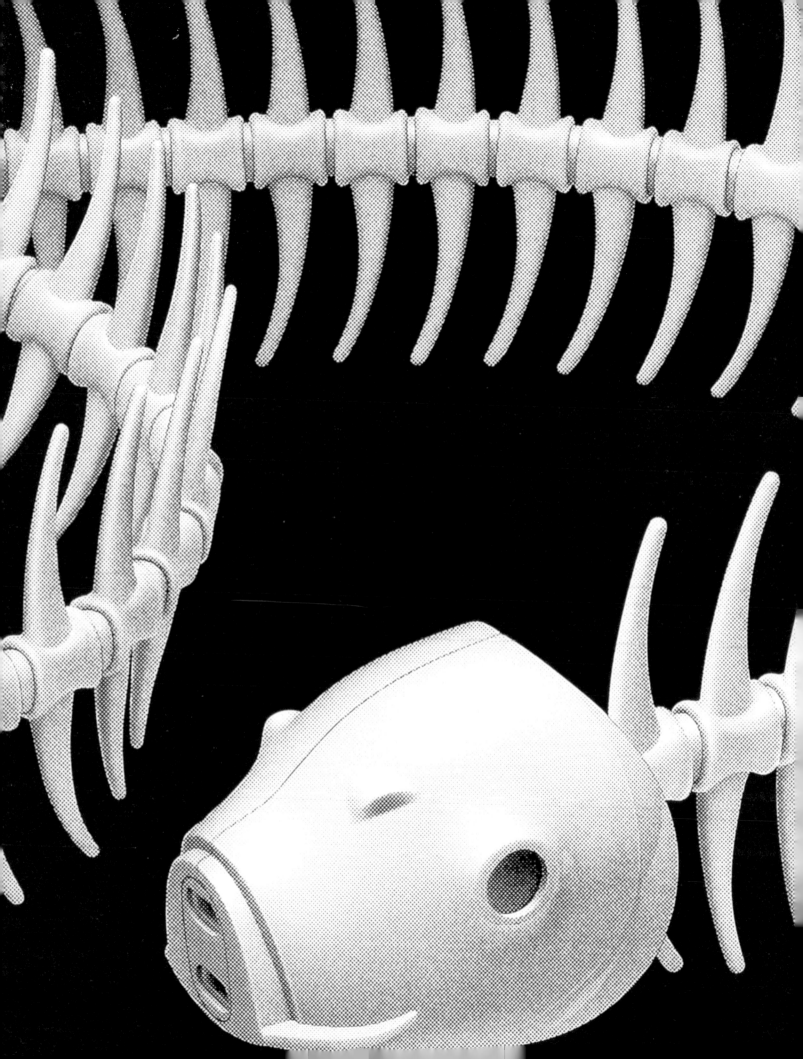

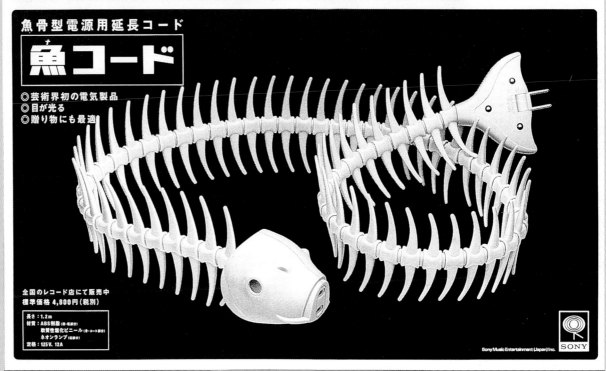

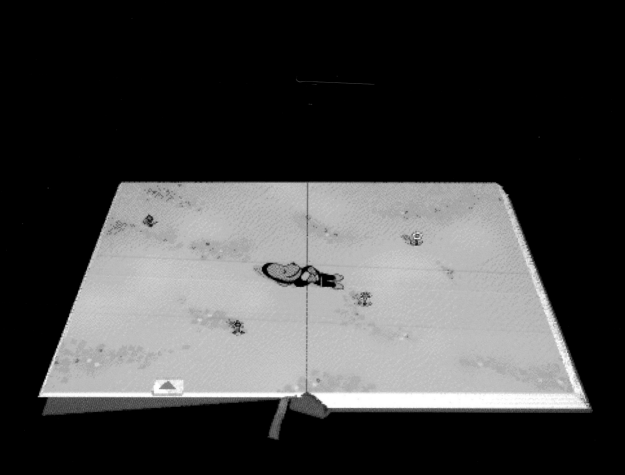

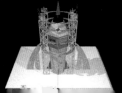
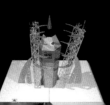
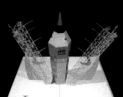
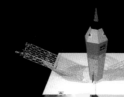
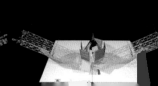

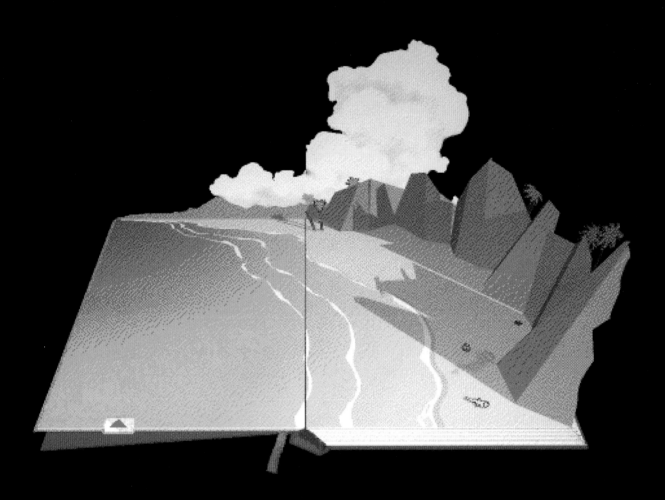

WITH INTERACTIVE MEDIA, THE EVENT REPLACES THE MEANING. INTERACTION REPLACES ANALYSIS, MEDITATIONS AND CONSCIOUS CHOICE. IT SUBSTITUTES PHYSICAL AND SENSORY ENGAGEMENT – PLEASURE AND PAIN. FOR EXAMPLE, WHAT DO YOU THINK WHEN YOU PLAY PLAYSTATION? AND: DO GAME SHOW CONTESTANTS TEND TOWARDS THE MEDITATIVE OR THE HYSTERICAL? IS JERRY SPRINGER CLOSER TO A PSYCHOANALYST OR A PSYCHOPATH? INTERACTIVE MEDIA RE-IMMERSES US IN THE PRIMORDIAL STEW OF PRE-CONSCIOUSNESS.

DIVE IN

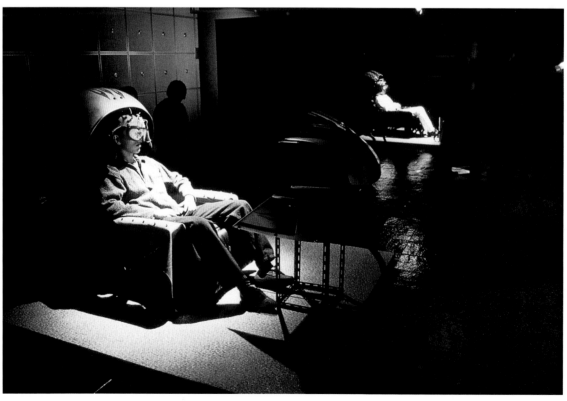

ON THIS SITE WILL RISE
A SHOPPING MALL

着せかえ人間 第1号

森村泰昌
アートディレクション=タナカノリユキ

定食

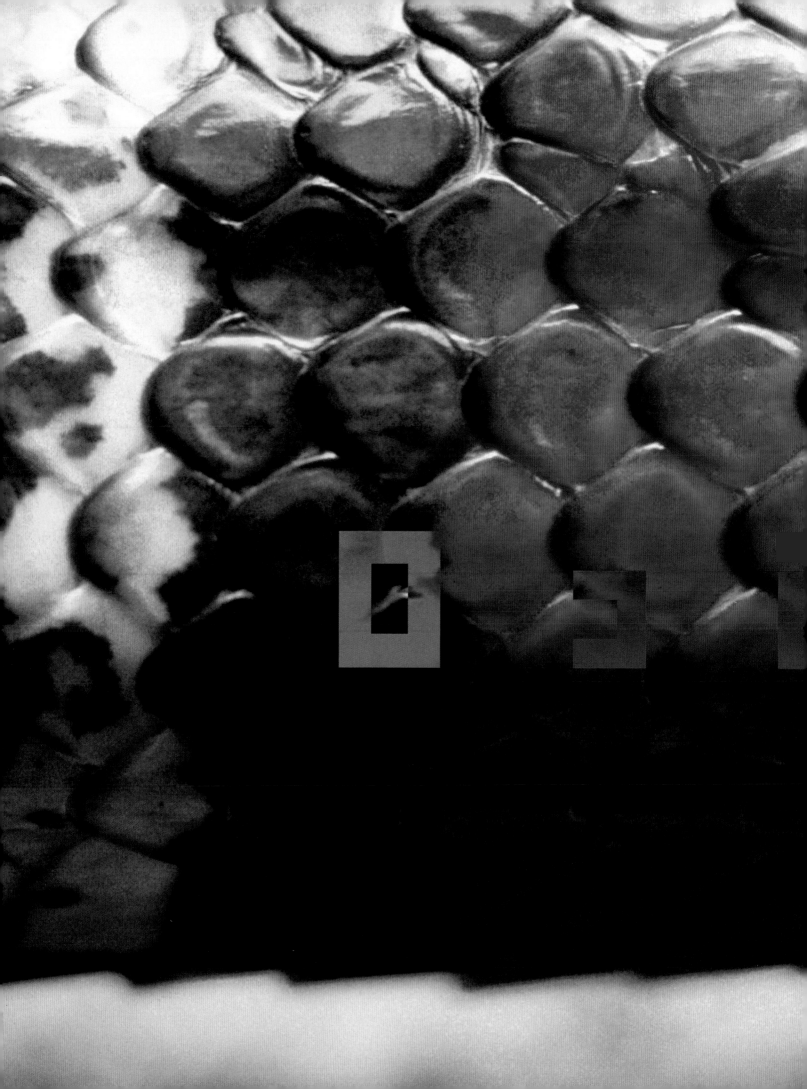

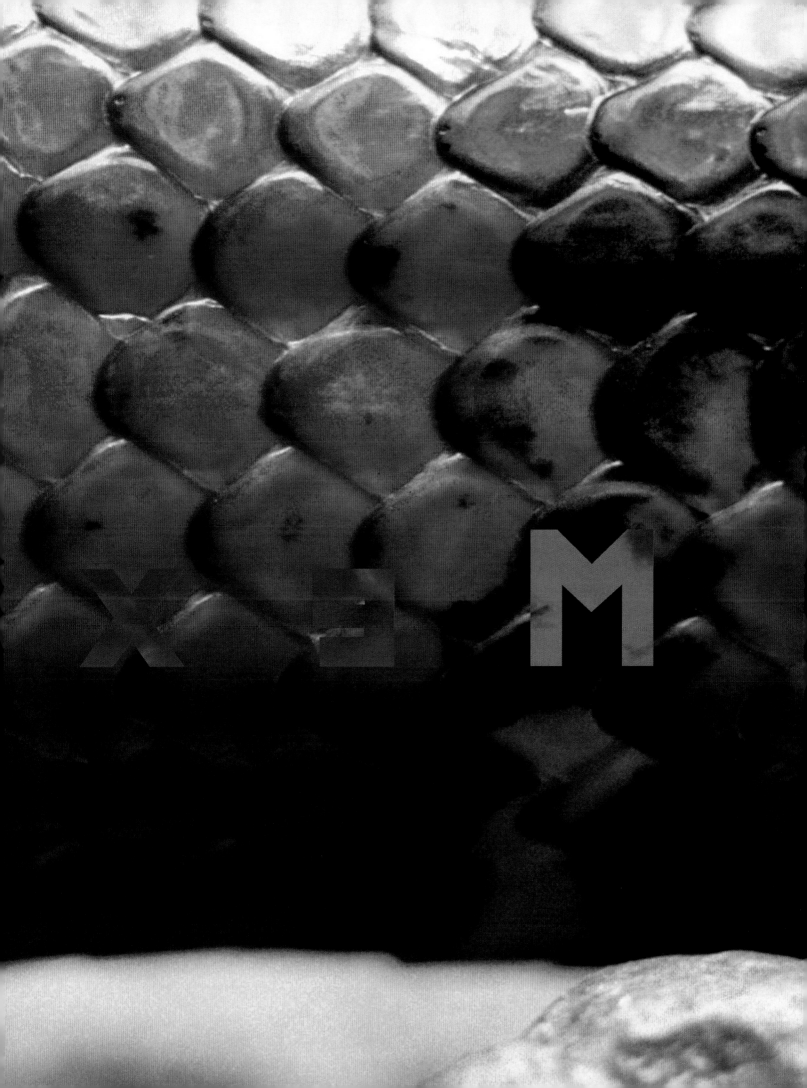

FAKIR

Revista tipo CHAMOY

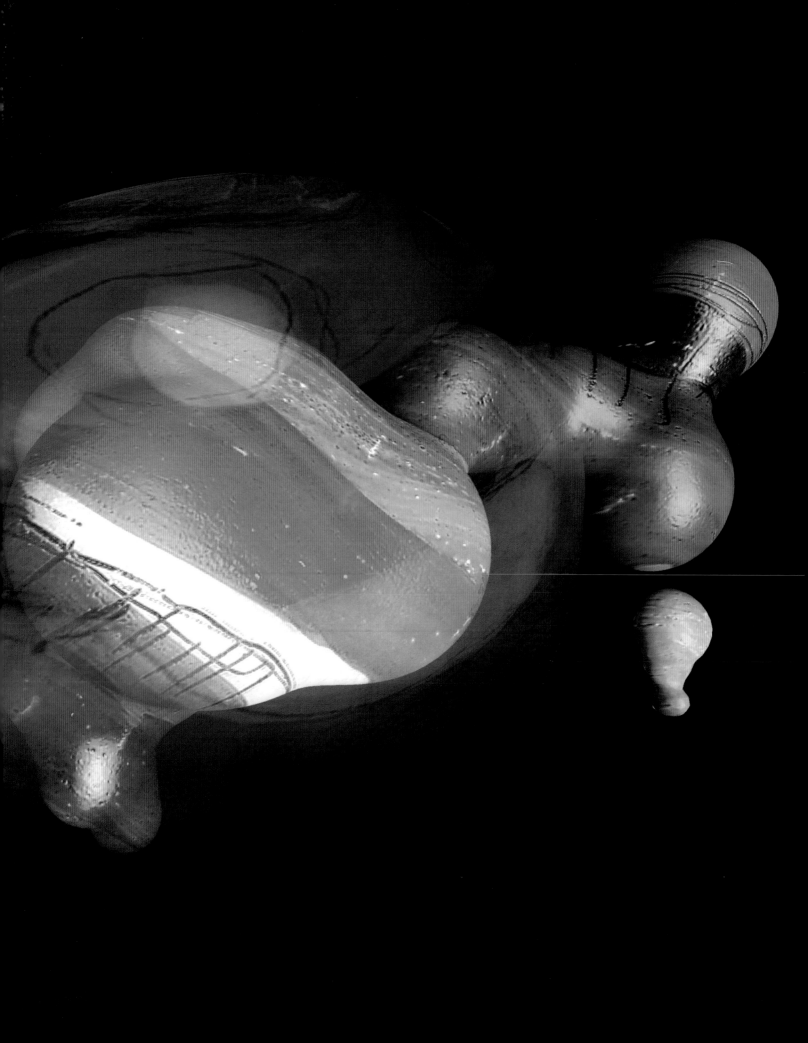

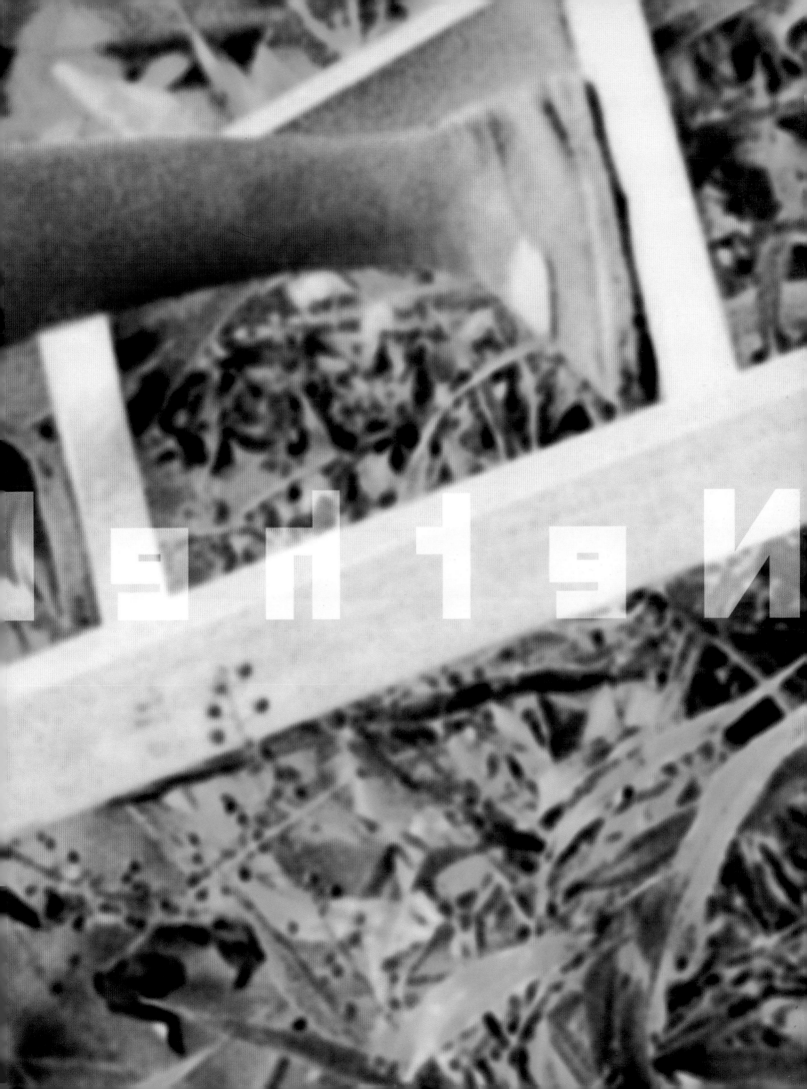

SHOCK

LET

DIENCE

DEF

LF

BOREDOM

TING

ING

UA ЗHT

INE

INE

ZTI

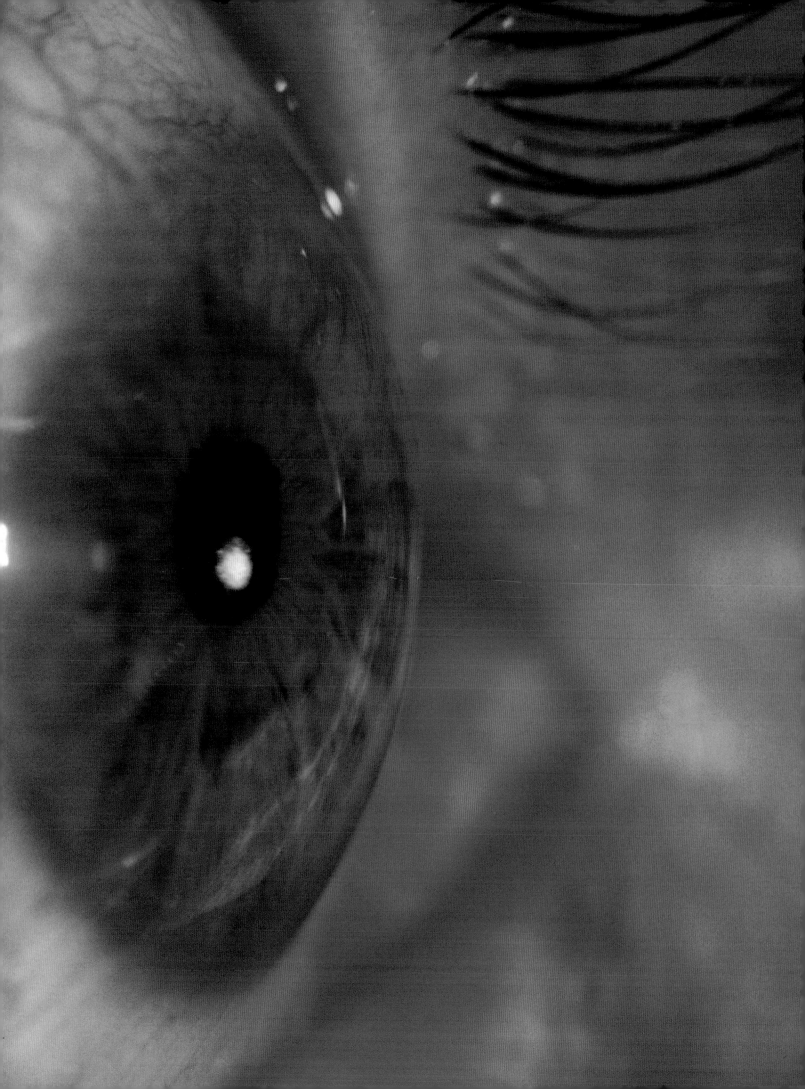

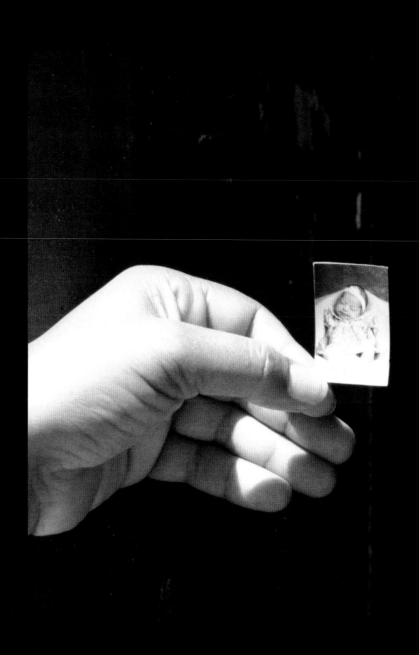

ACIDITY

IS THE BLESSING FOR THE PEOPLE

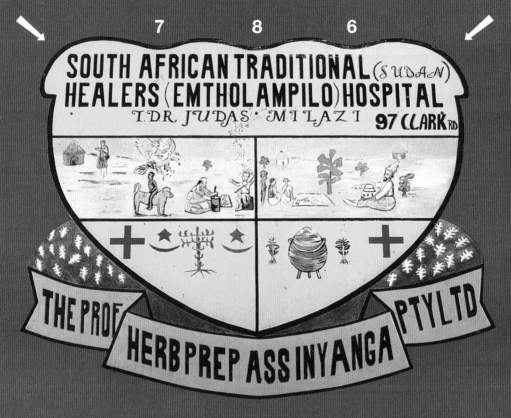

7 8 6

SOUTH AFRICAN TRADITIONAL (SUDAN) HEALERS (EMTHOLAMPILO) HOSPITAL

T.DR. JUDAS • MILAZI 97 CLARK RD

THE PROF HERB PREP ASS INYANGA PTY LTD

WITch DocteR WhicH DocteR?

Muti Power

Full Knowledge of Sickness

MANAGER. B.A. NGWAZI ☎. 305 5719

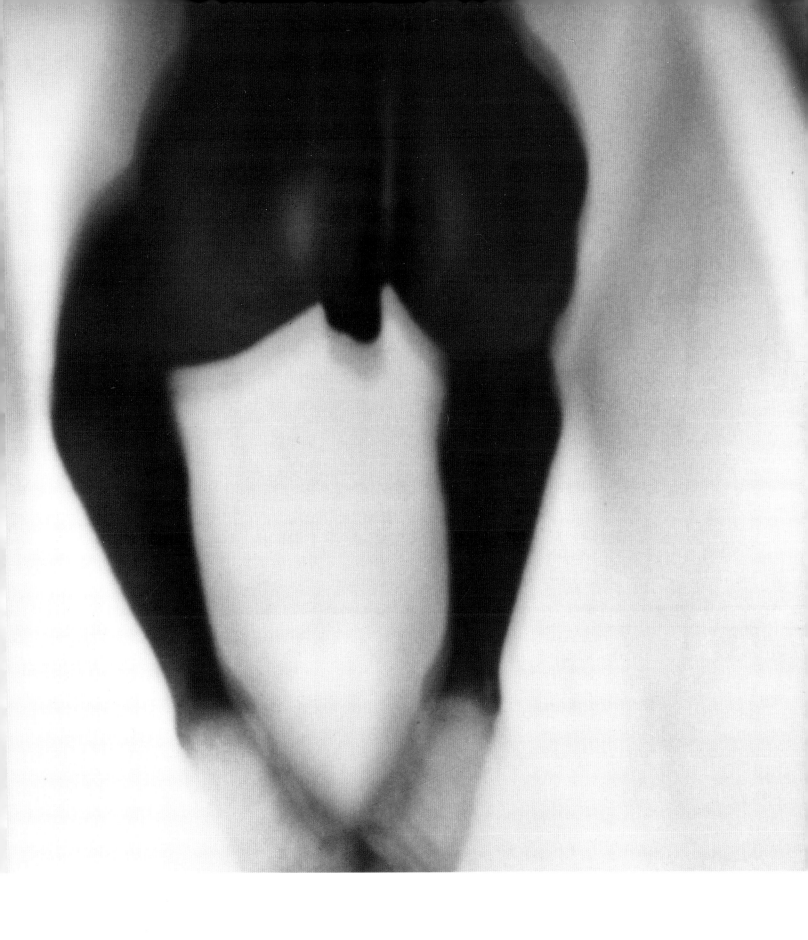

SHO
SEDUCTION

DCK OR ASSAULT

ARE WE AT OUR MOST DIRECT, OUR MOST EMOTIVE, WHEN WE LOCK INTO PRE-LINGUISTIC COMMUNICATION?

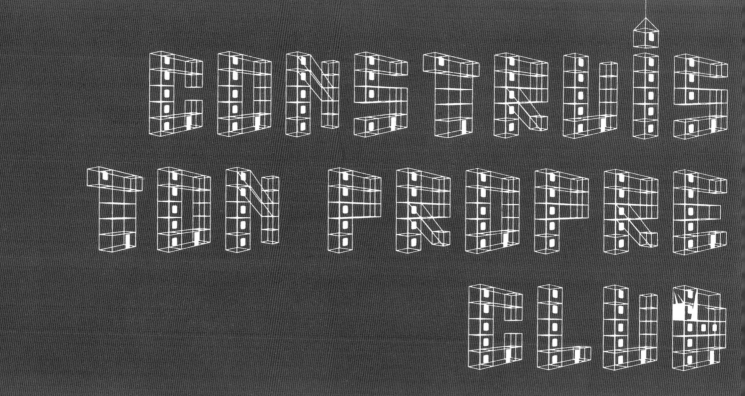

CONSTRUIS TON PROPRE CLUB

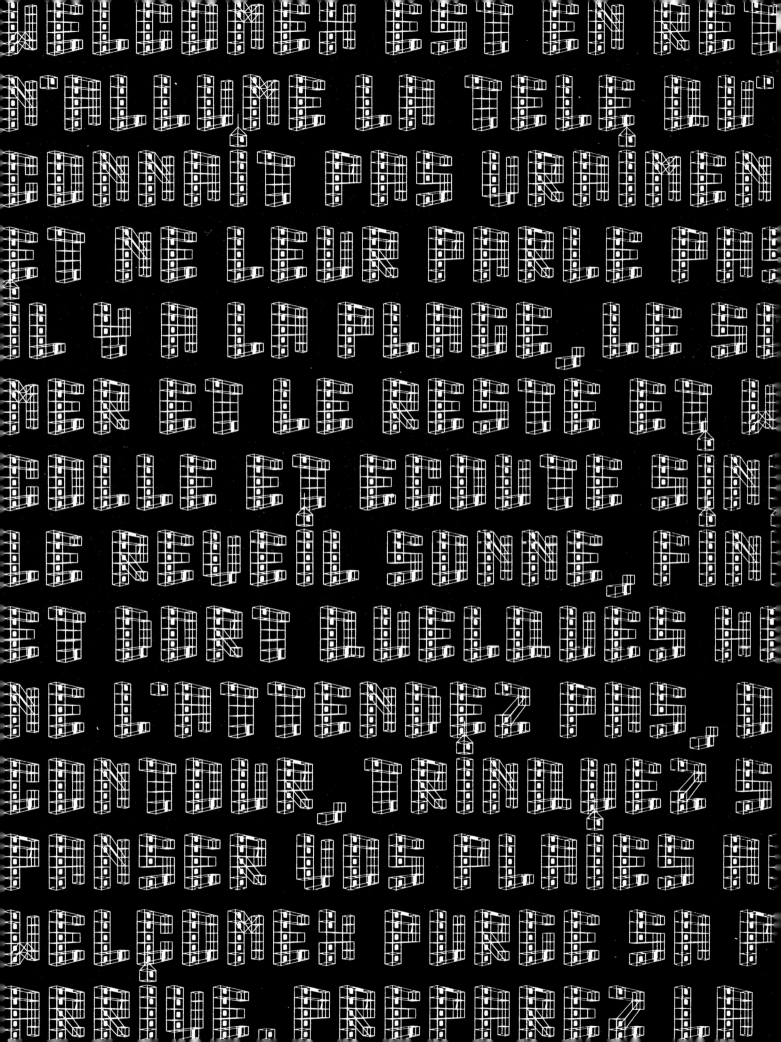

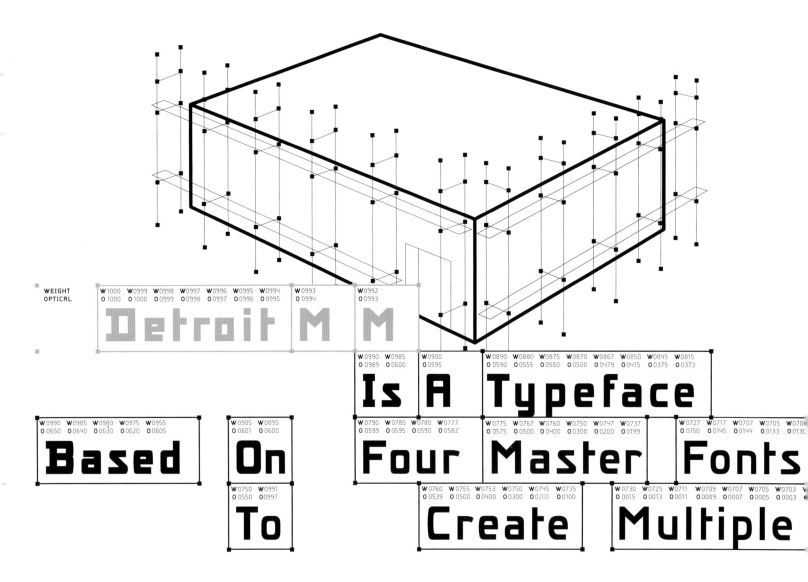

WEIGHT
OPTICAL

W 1000	W 0999	W 0998	W 0997	W 0996	W 0995	W 0994	W 0993	W 0992
O 1000	O 1000	O 0999	O 0998	O 0997	O 0996	O 0995	O 0994	O 0993

Detroit M M

W 0990	W 0985	W 0900	W 0890	W 0880	W 0875	W 0870	W 0867	W 0850	W 0845	W 0815
O 0989	O 0600	O 0595	O 0590	O 0555	O 0550	O 0500	O 0479	O 0415	O 0375	O 0373

Is A Typeface

W 0990	W 0985	W 0980	W 0975	W 0955
O 0650	O 0640	O 0630	O 0620	O 0605

Based

W 0905	W 0895
O 0601	O 0600

On

W 0790	W 0785	W 0780	W 0777	W 0775	W 0767	W 0760	W 0750	W 0747	W 0737	W 0727	W 0717	W 0707	W 0705	W 070
O 0599	O 0595	O 0590	O 0582	O 0575	O 0500	O 0400	O 0300	O 0200	O 0199	O 0150	O 0145	O 0144	O 0133	O 0130

Four Master Fonts

W 0750	W 0991
O 0550	O 0997

To

W 0760	W 0755	W 0753	W 0750	W 0745	W 0735	W 0730	W 0725	W 0711	W 0709	W 0707	W 0705	W 0703
O 0539	O 0500	O 0400	O 0300	O 0200	O 0100	O 0015	O 0013	O 0011	O 0009	O 0007	O 0005	O 0003

Create Multiple

W 0700
O 0010

&

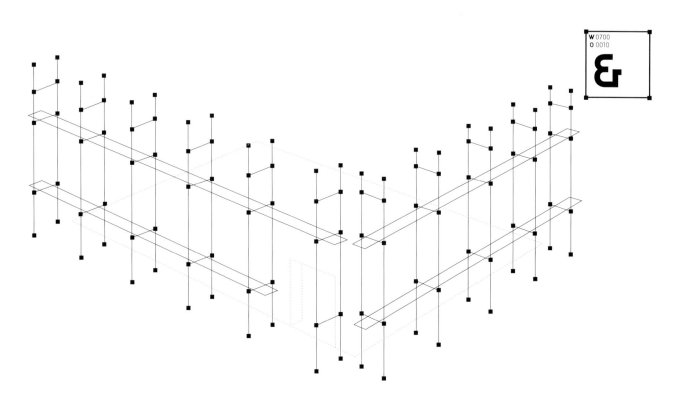

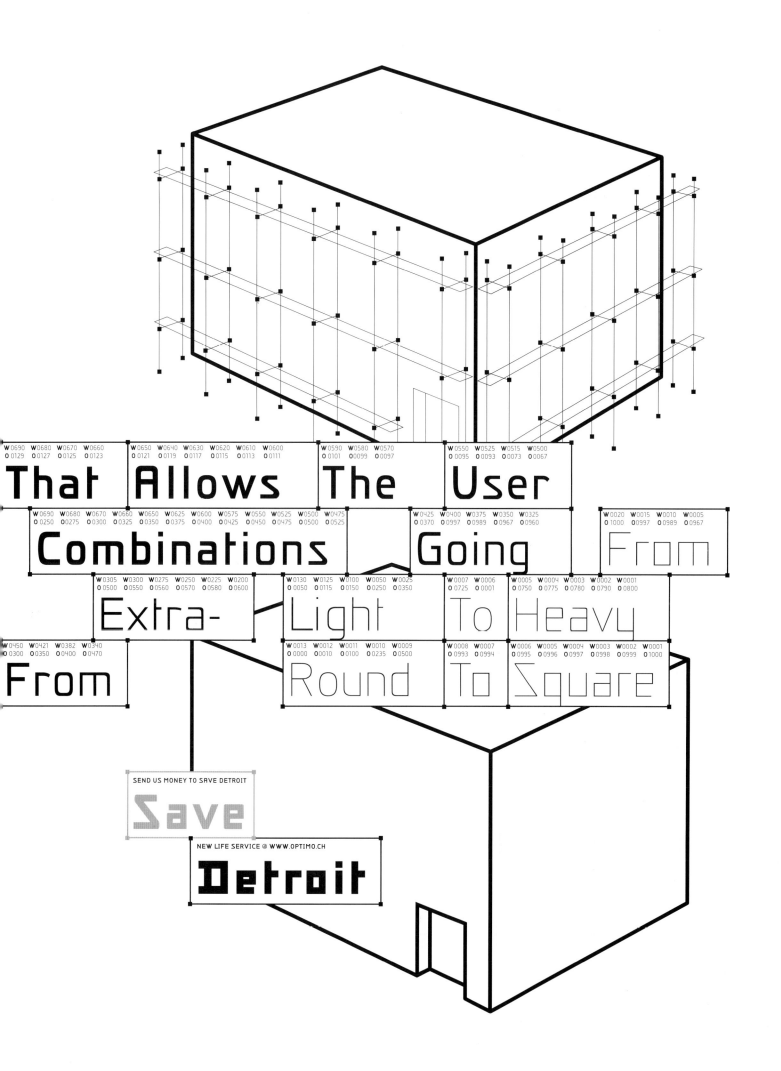

W 0690 O 0129	W 0680 O 0127	W 0670 O 0125	W 0660 O 0123		W 0650 O 0121	W 0640 O 0119	W 0630 O 0117	W 0620 O 0115	W 0610 O 0113	W 0600 O 0111		W 0590 O 0101	W 0580 O 0099	W 0570 O 0097		W 0550 O 0095	W 0525 O 0093	W 0515 O 0073	W 0500 O 0067

That Allows The User

W 0690 O 0250	W 0680 O 0275	W 0670 O 0300	W 0660 O 0325	W 0650 O 0350	W 0625 O 0375	W 0600 O 0400	W 0575 O 0425	W 0550 O 0450	W 0525 O 0475	W 0500 O 0500	W 0475 O 0525	W 0425 O 0370	W 0400 O 0997	W 0375 O 0989	W 0350 O 0967	W 0325 O 0960	W 0020 O 1000	W 0015 O 0997	W 0010 O 0989	W 0005 O 0967

Combinations Going From

W 0305 O 0500	W 0300 O 0550	W 0275 O 0560	W 0250 O 0570	W 0225 O 0580	W 0200 O 0600	W 0130 O 0050	W 0125 O 0115	W 0100 O 0150	W 0050 O 0250	W 0025 O 0350	W 0007 O 0725	W 0006 O 0001	W 0005 O 0750	W 0004 O 0775	W 0003 O 0780	W 0002 O 0790	W 0001 O 0800

Extra- Light To Heavy

W 0450 O 0300	W 0421 O 0350	W 0382 O 0400	W 0340 O 0470	W 0013 O 0000	W 0012 O 0010	W 0011 O 0100	W 0010 O 0235	W 0009 O 0500	W 0008 O 0993	W 0007 O 0994	W 0006 O 0995	W 0005 O 0996	W 0004 O 0997	W 0003 O 0998	W 0002 O 0999	W 0001 O 1000

From Round To Square

SEND US MONEY TO SAVE DETROIT

Save

NEW LIFE SERVICE @ WWW.OPTIMO.CH

Detroit

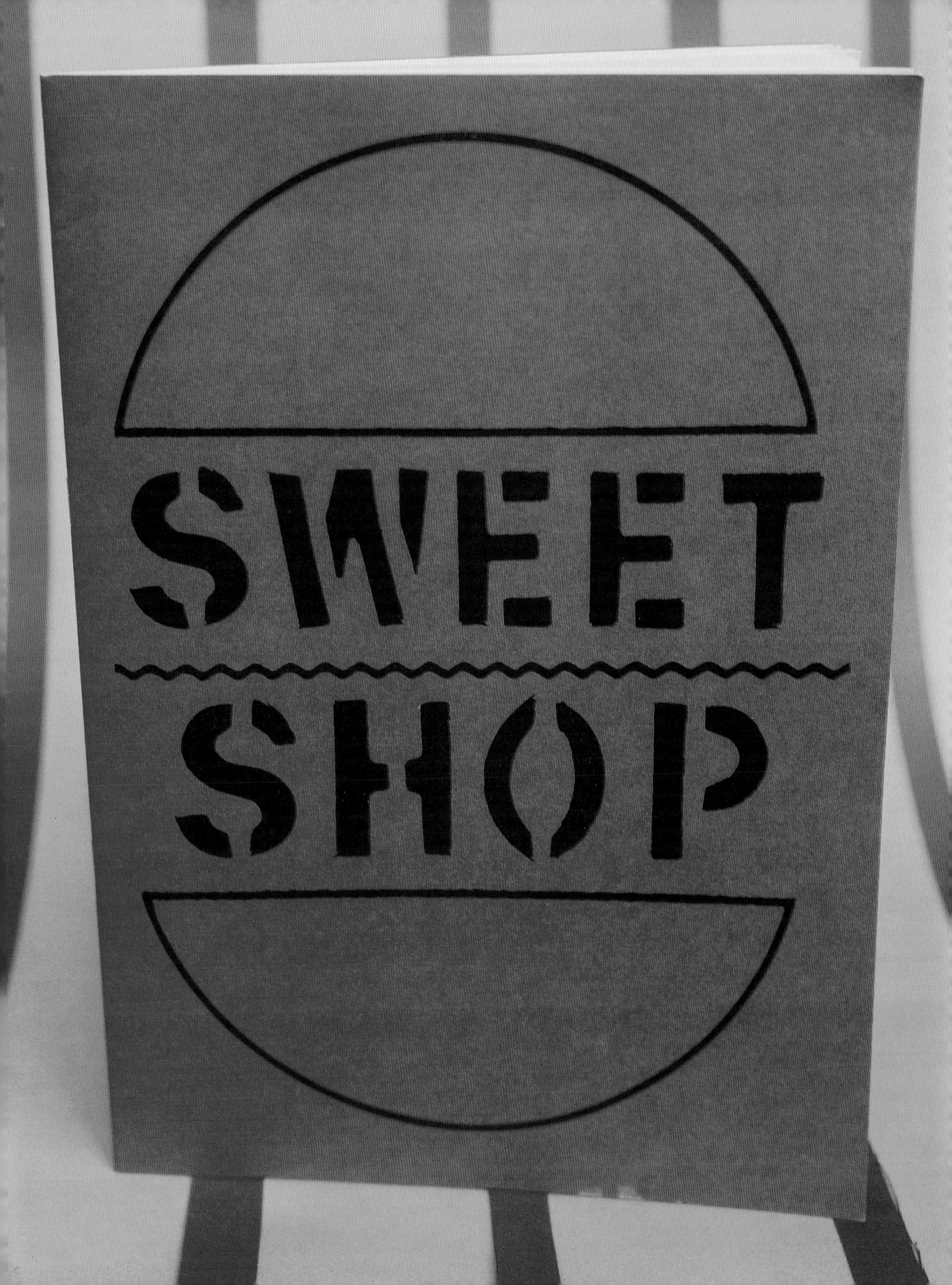
SWEET
SHOP

FLASH

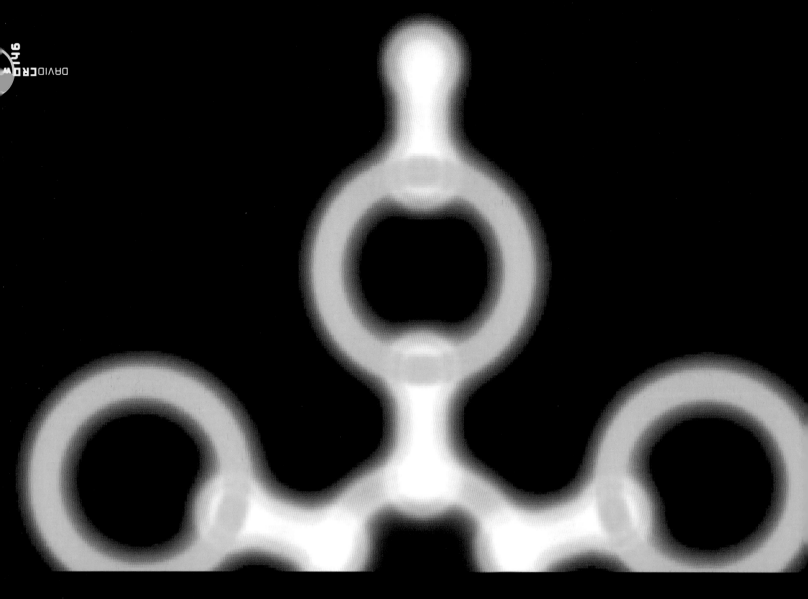

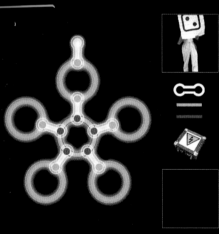

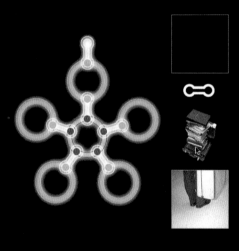

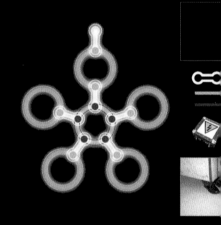

departure

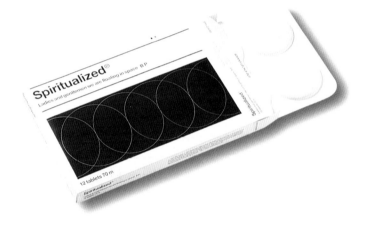

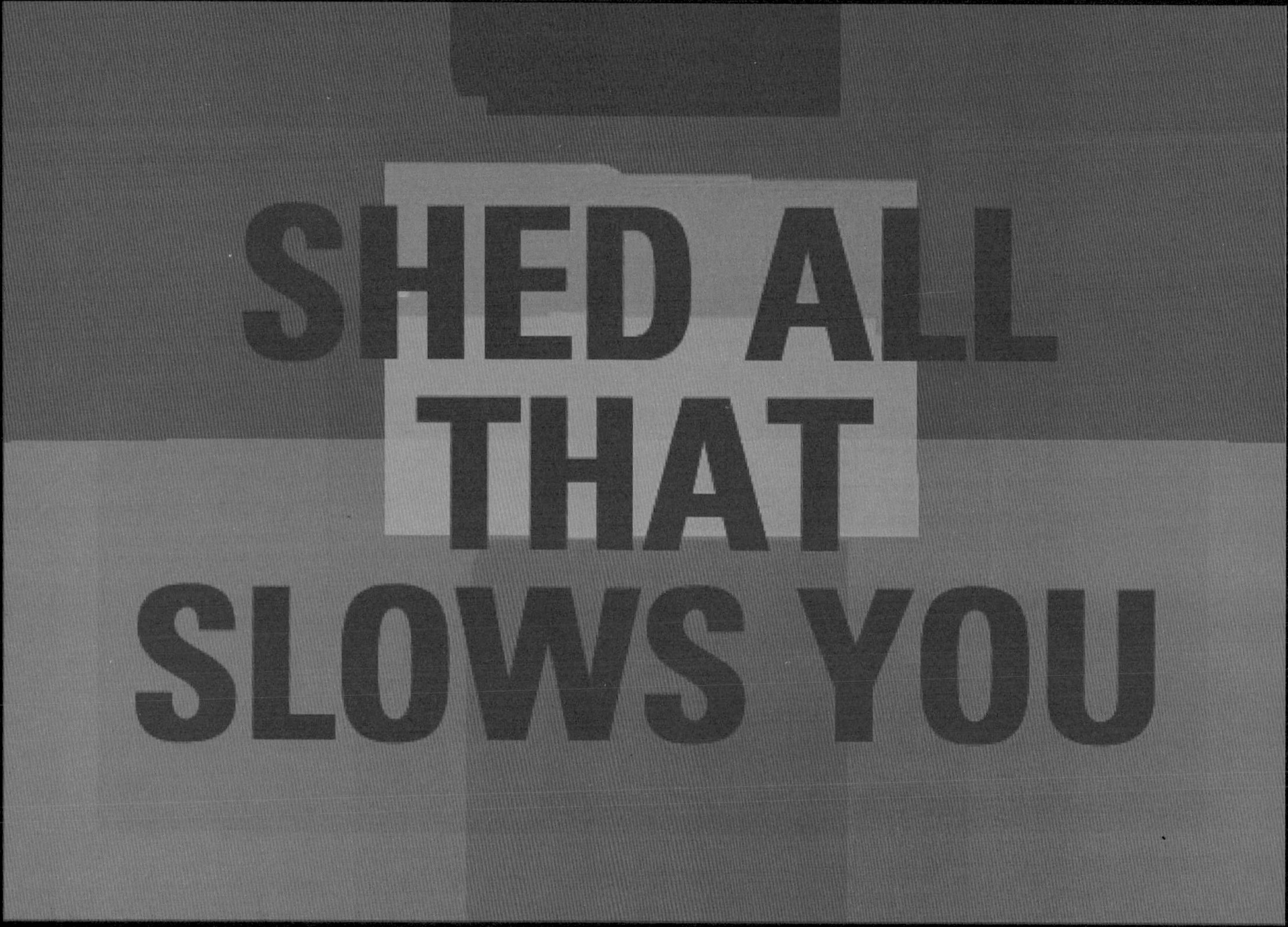
SHED ALL
THAT
SLOWS YOU

ALL
THAT
HOLDS
YOU

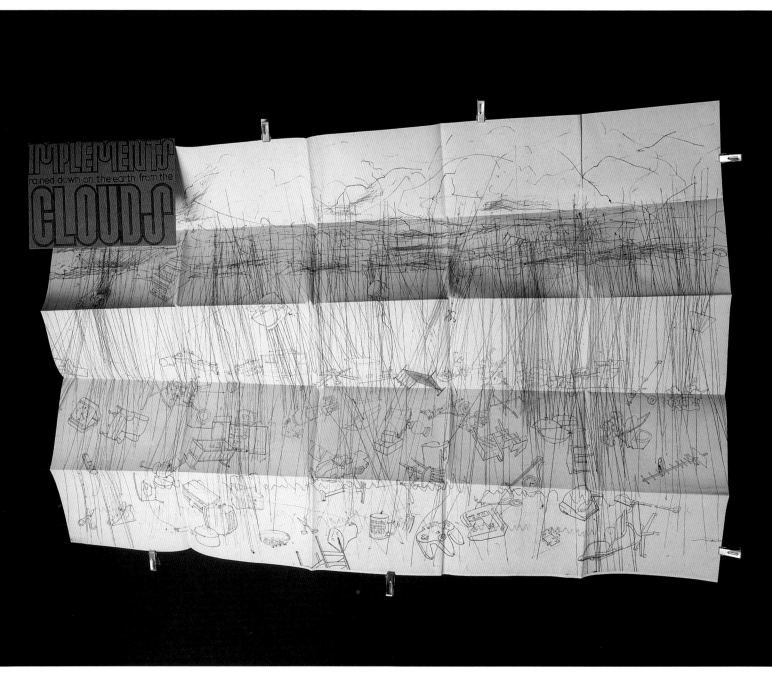

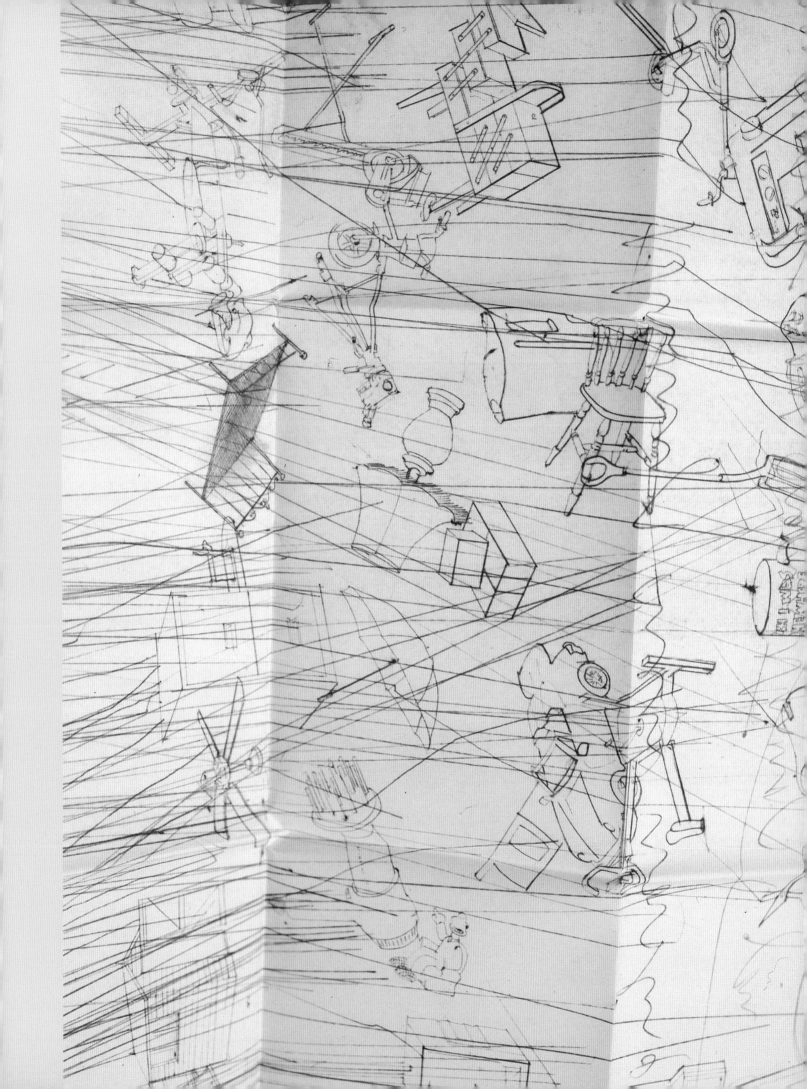

NOTHING HAPPENS HERE

THIS IS THE STILL POINT AT THE CENTRE

BETWEEN

YOUR DREAM OF THE CREATOR

+

YOUR CONCEPTION OF SELF

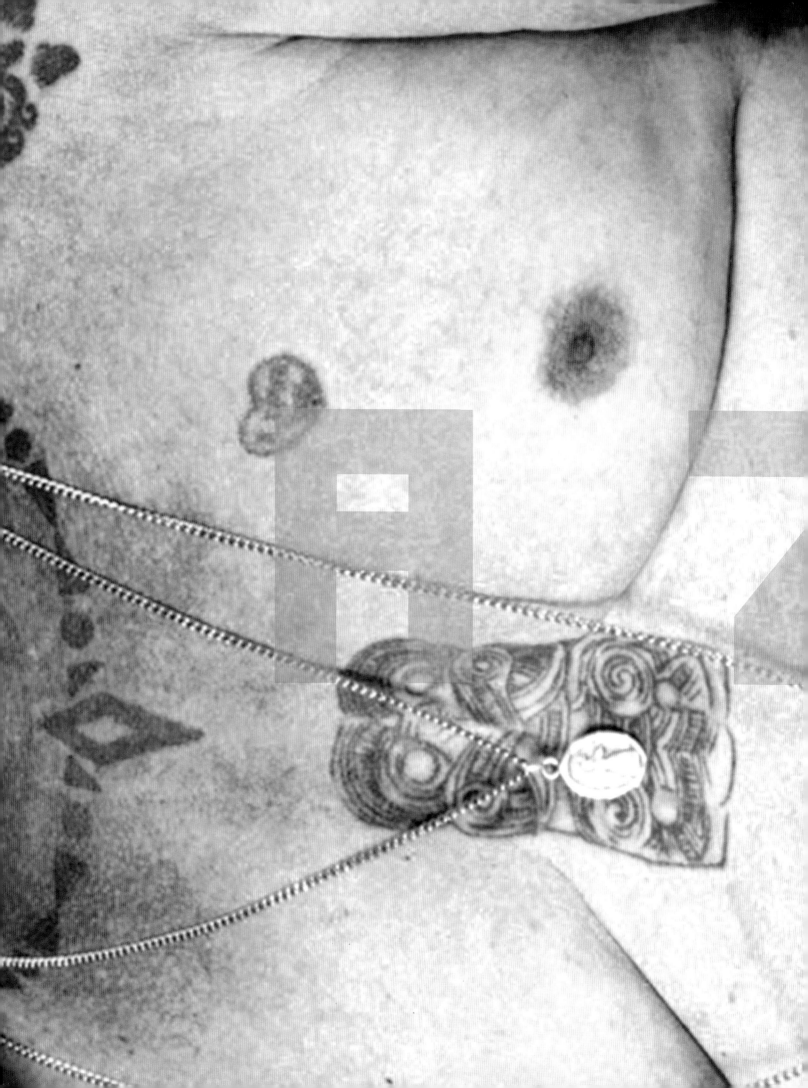

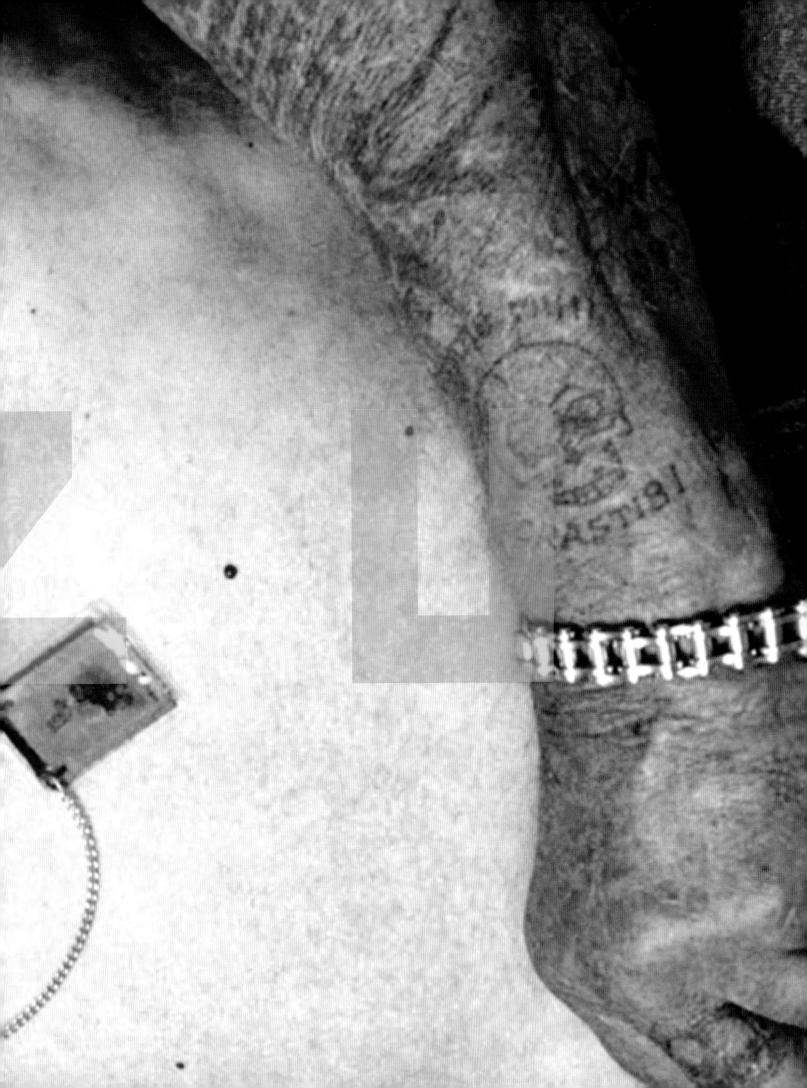

BARK
Little
Doggie

Y DOES IT F∃

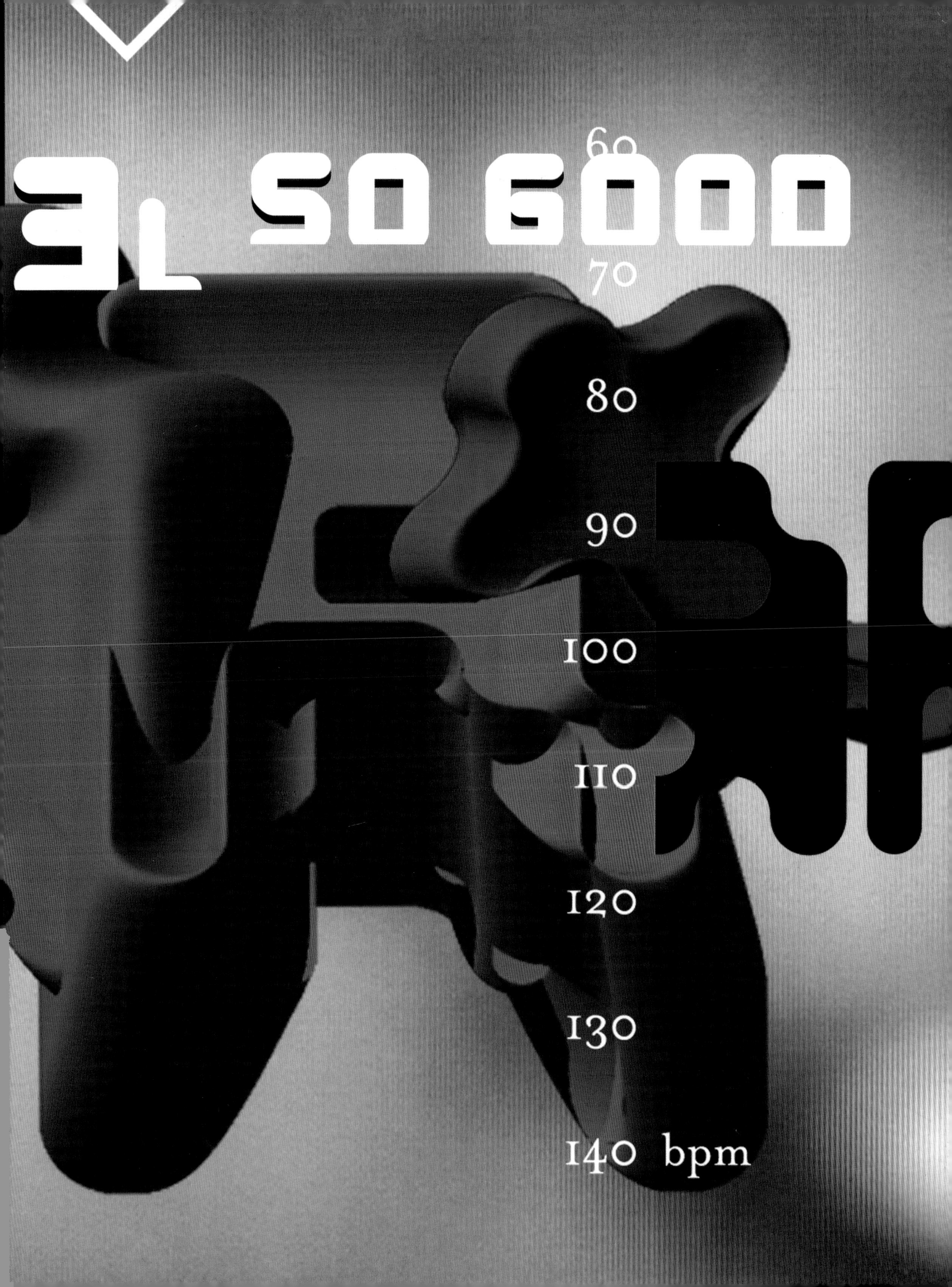
SO GOOD
60
70
80
90
100
110
120
130
140 bpm

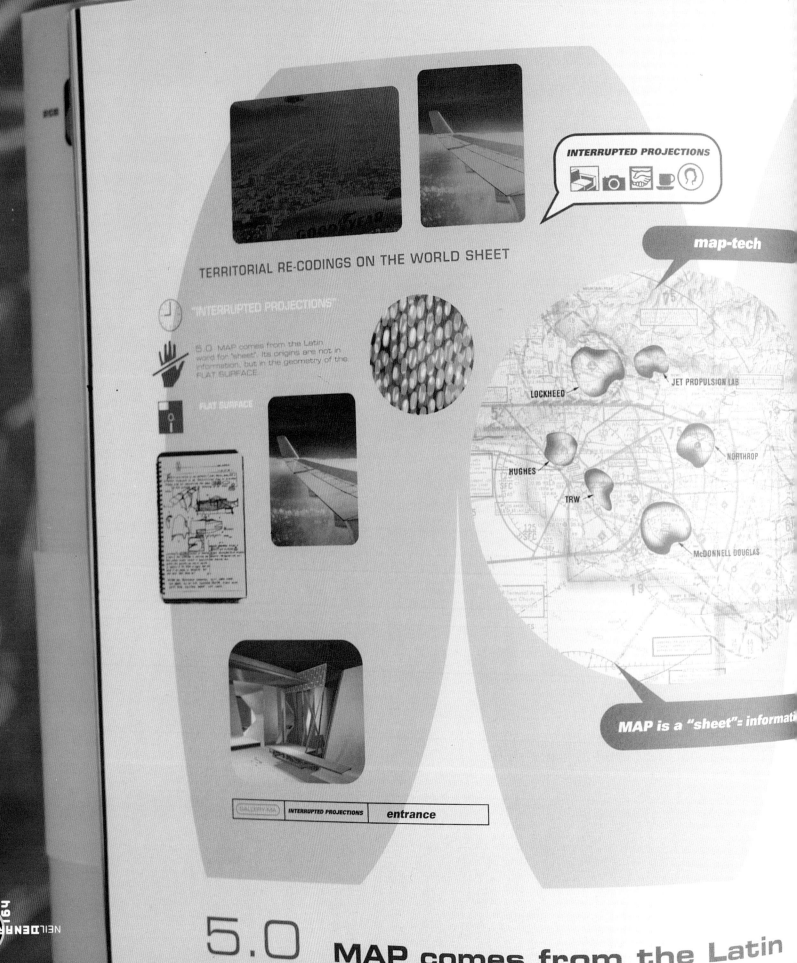

TERRITORIAL RE-CODINGS ON THE WORLD SHEET

"INTERRUPTED PROJECTIONS"

5.0 MAP comes from the Latin word for "sheet". Its origins are not in information, but in the geometry of the FLAT SURFACE.

FLAT SURFACE

INTERRUPTED PROJECTIONS

INTERRUPTED PROJECTIONS

map-tech

LOCKHEED

JET PROPULSION LAB

NORTHROP

HUGHES

TRW

McDONNELL DOUGLAS

MAP is a "sheet"= informati

GALLERY MA | INTERRUPTED PROJECTIONS | entrance

5.0 MAP comes from the Latin word for "sheet". Its origins are not information, but in the geometry of t

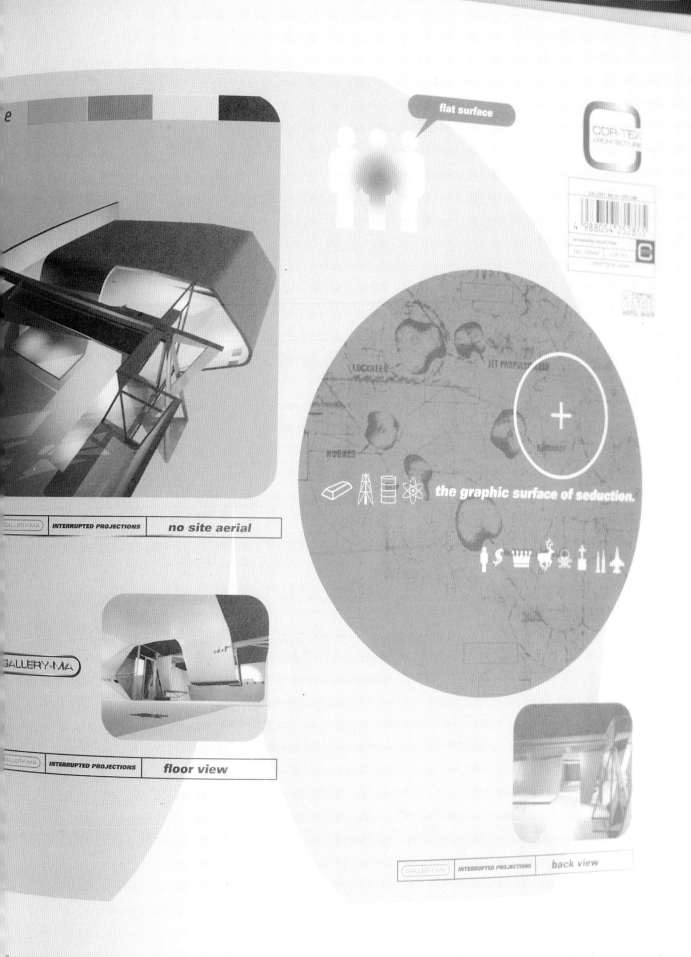

flat surface

COR-TEX
ARCHITECTURE

the graphic surface of seduction.

GALLERY·MA | INTERRUPTED PROJECTIONS | *no site aerial*

GALLERY·MA

GALLERY·MA | INTERRUPTED PROJECTIONS | *floor view*

GALLERY·MA | INTERRUPTED PROJECTIONS | *back view*

5.0 MAP comes from the Latin word for "sheet". Its origins are not in information, but in the geometry of the FLAT SURFACE.
As a 2D plane, the sheet must be bent in order to architecturally spatialize a phenomenon. Its flatness is overcome by the powerful ability for architecture to momentarily intensify the graphic surface of seduction. ▶ P76

that's why I LIKE it here with you
in between THE where
and the THE
here

(cough))

pan to the left—————
YOU'RE AT AT THE CENTER
pan to the right—
there you are again

AT THE CENTER
making things happen

IT'S LIKE BEING AT THE CIRCUS WITH YOU
we're watching quintuplet tight rope walkers
they're smiling back
we're balancing them with our collective gaze
I think they almost feel it

dead in the eye
the panoptic feedback LLOOPP dilating
themassMediascape ... ...
"our" Main Street, a thousand miles across
see you at Borders©
or some other bookseller pushing expensive
coffee & designer fetish

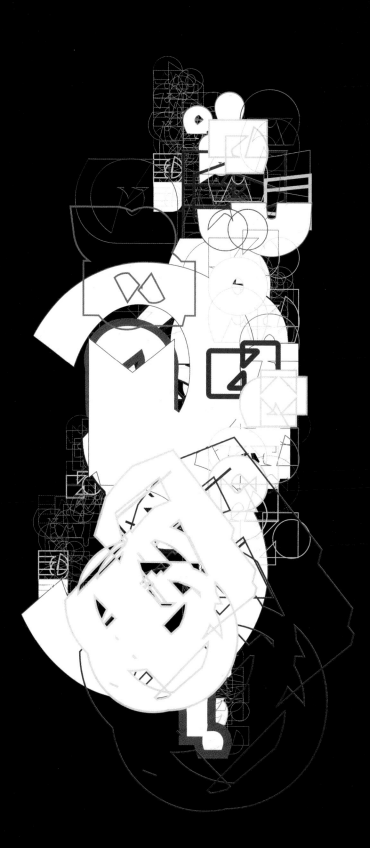

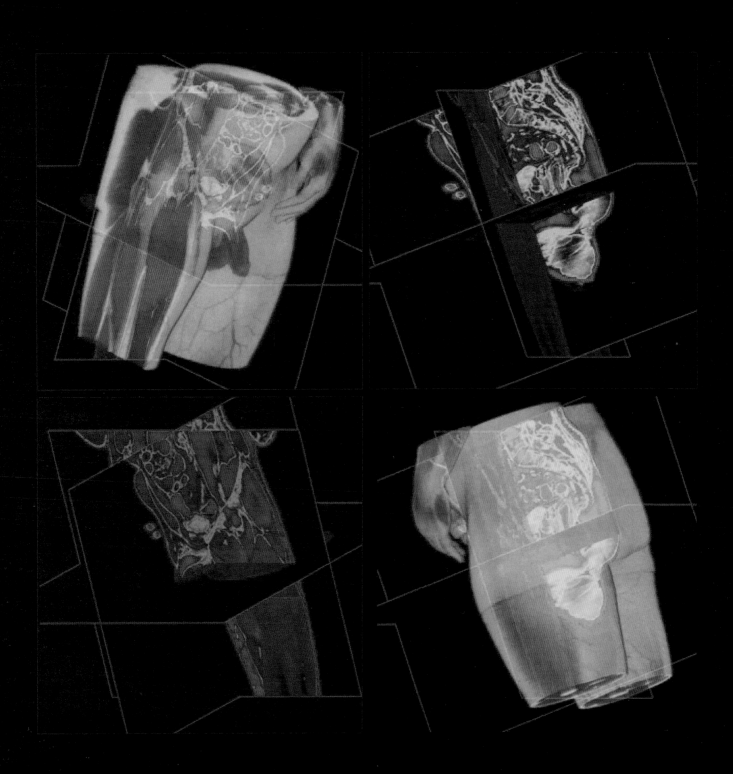

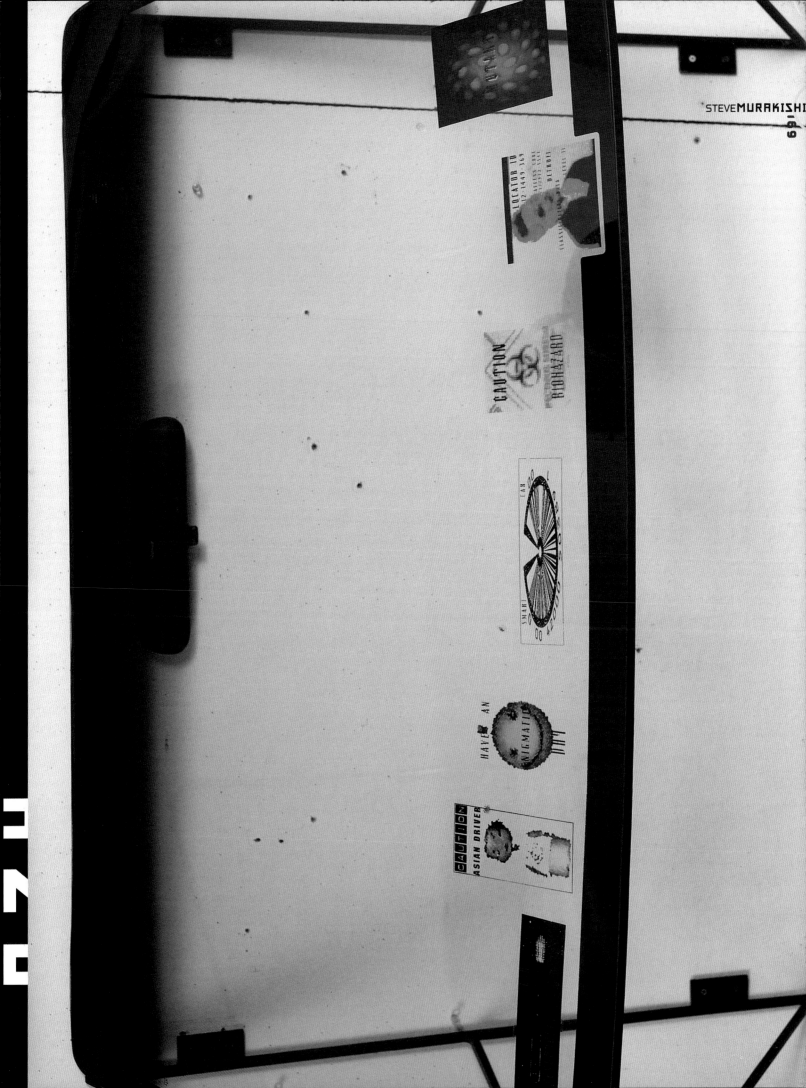

ACCOMM

MASS

REQUIR

ASSIM

ANNIH

MEANING

MEDIA

ESUS TO

MODATE

ILATE

ILATE

DIFFERENCE

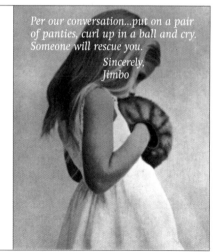

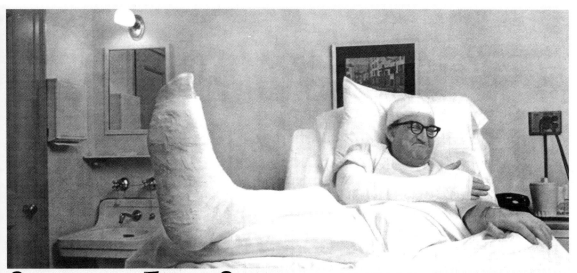

introducing the Worlds First
plaster of paris dog shit unitard
With two fisted exertion cups and suspiciously hardened lambskin rinse cycles!

In a world of clandestine appointments, sepia pecks and collusionist crotch flags you know there's a keeper who's a keeper. With legs akimbo and a metallic after taste, we'll parley our latest windfall into your pre-nuptial foolhardy stink matt without missing a beat. NOW THAT'S A LESION WE CAN ALL LIVE WITH!

🏠 Teen Heritage Exertion Cups

4.

LOOK WHO PUT THE
Waldorf Pissing Vest™
BACK ONTO CROTCH
QUAKE RANDOLPH

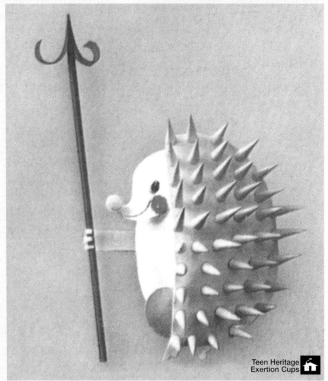

Teen Heritage Exertion Cups 🏠

5.

Supply&demanD®

6.

Cabbage Patch BURN VICTIM™ 7.

1.
ART DIRECTOR : Rob Strong
COPY WRITER : Mike Athens
ARTIST: Tim Colfax
PHOTOGRAPHER: Steve Wagstaff
CLIENT: Saddle Sores
AGENCY: Andersen Kluth Messiah

2.
ART DIRECTOR : Philip Daniels
COPY WRITER : Barry Wasserman
ARTIST: Carl Berman
PHOTOGRAPHER: Jack Braithwaite
CLIENT: Fumes McCoy
AGENCY: Windsor Tapscott &
Everette/BDDQ

3.
ART DIRECTOR : Rob Justin
COPY WRITER : Carl DePew
PHOTOGRAPHER: Matt Walters
CLIENT: Sloppy Barn Lessons
AGENCY: Jaspar Wentworth Cables

4.
ART DIRECTOR : Dale Jergunsen
COPY WRITER : Mike Athens
ARTIST: Bill Hubbard
PHOTOGRAPHER: Jerry Lansing
CLIENT: Teen Heritage Exertion Cups
AGENCY: Andersen Kluth Messiah

5.
ART DIRECTOR : Dale Jergunsen
COPY WRITER : Mike Athens
ARTIST: Bill Hubbard
PHOTOGRAPHER: Jerry Lansing
CLIENT: Teen Heritage Exertion Cups
AGENCY: Andersen Kluth Messiah

6.
ART DIRECTOR : Tim Saunders
COPY WRITER : Gregg DeMuth
ARTIST: Havier Valdez
PHOTOGRAPHER: Lance Oppenheim
CLIENT: Supply&Demand
AGENCY: TTB&E

7.
ART DIRECTOR : Roger Walker
ARTIST: Colgate Studios
CLIENT: Cabbage Patch Burn Victim
AGENCY: Olsen Hendricks

have their own personality. They become their ow[n]
when I go on auditions, you become protective, a[nd]
personally, when someone doesn't like your feet,
Sometimes it gets way over the top, and you thin[k]
my feelings are so hurt, my feet didn't get this job
of have a reality check on it.

AM: So it's pretty competitive?
ES: Yes, like any part of the modeling industry. Th[ere are]
people who are really doing it, so you really know
most of the time. And some of the jobs are very hi[gh]
becomes quite competitive.

AM: So v
MR: It's f[i]
hand up
hand. Th[e]
if you ar[e]
foot and
of it, I'm
strength,
there, be
and vasc[ular]

AM: So are the top foot models ten people, twe[nty?]
ES: Probably about ten people. Not even ten people
who are really doing a lot of hands. There are prob[ably]
who are doing feet.

AM: Do you have a preferred shoe manufacturer
ES: Keds or Dr. Scholl's.

AM: When you have to wear high heels, do you e[ver]
ES: No, it's a scary experience. I get so freaked out a[bout]
high heels that I don't enjoy it. I got married in little
sneakers.

AM: Are
where w
MR: Rem[e]
a beach?
foot and
I remem[ber]
there's t[he]

AM: Lace sneakers?
ES: Yes, little white eyelet sneakers with lace bows.

AM: Wha[t]
MR: I've

AM: Are
MR: Sure
on your

AM: Do
MR: Inst[e]
toe. I te[nd]
all the t[i]
larger ar
If I'm go
I'll put a

AM: Do
MR: I be
reflexol[ogy]
in a cert
am float
like my

AM: Wh
MR: Dor

AM: Ha[ve]
MR: No
my feet

58   60

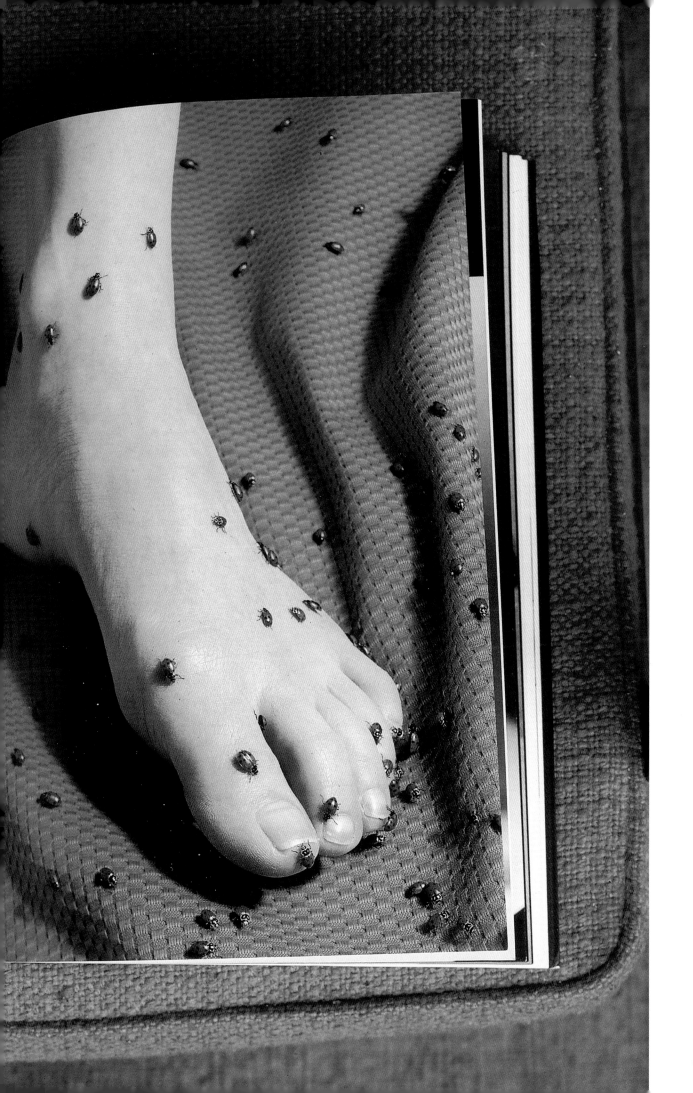

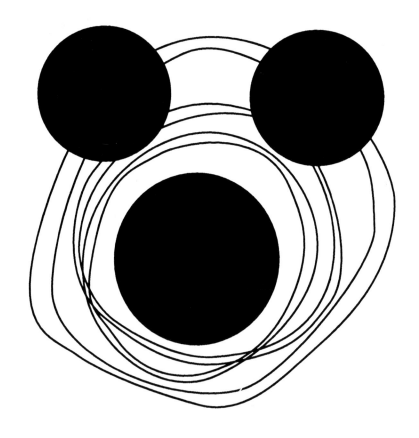

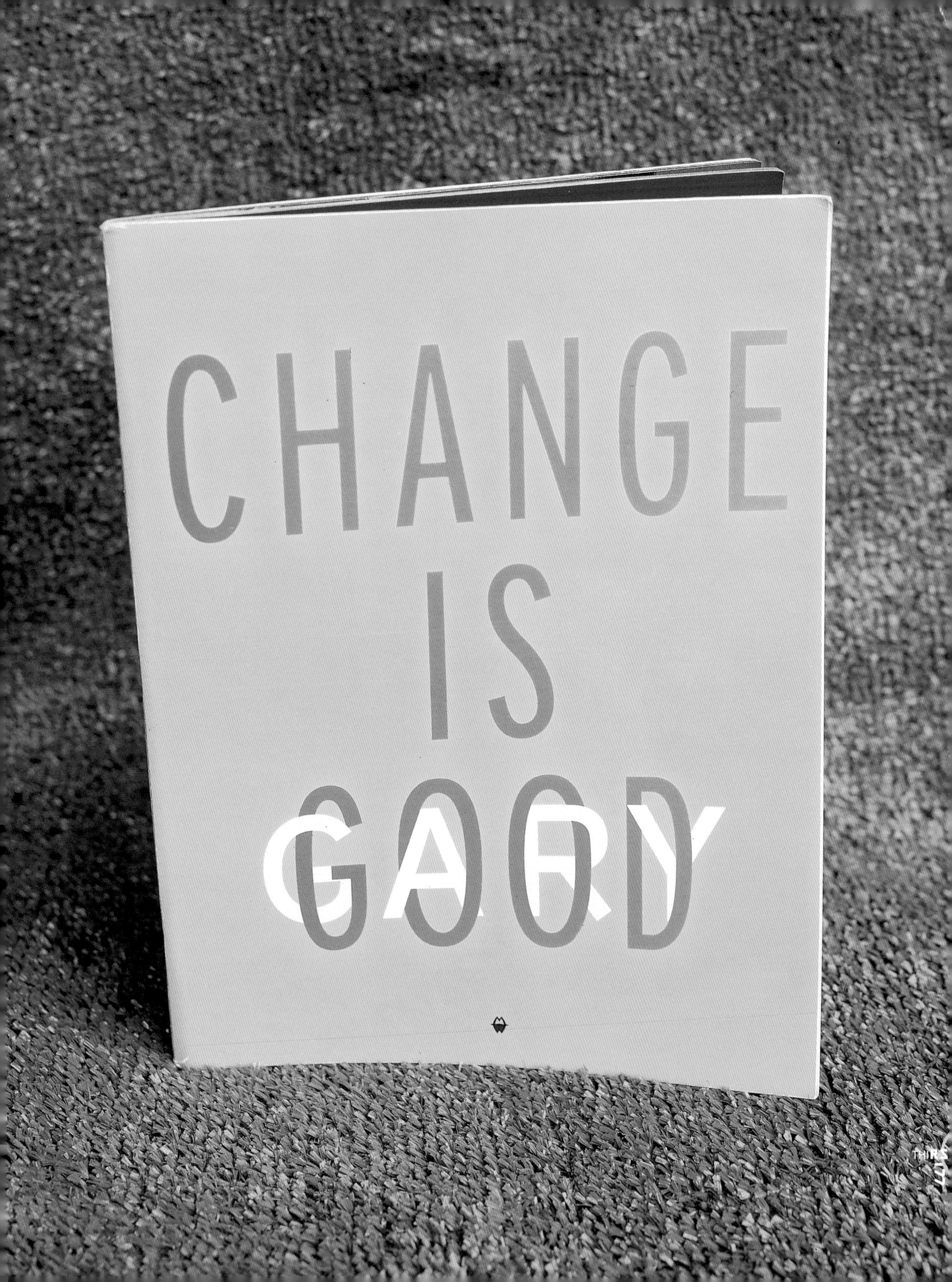
CHANGE
IS
GOOD
GARY

"good design" ☞ mas...

☞ style ☞

☞ interesting ☞

...estival ☞

market ☞ cliché ☞ embarrassment ☞ "it's a cliché?" ☞ fetish

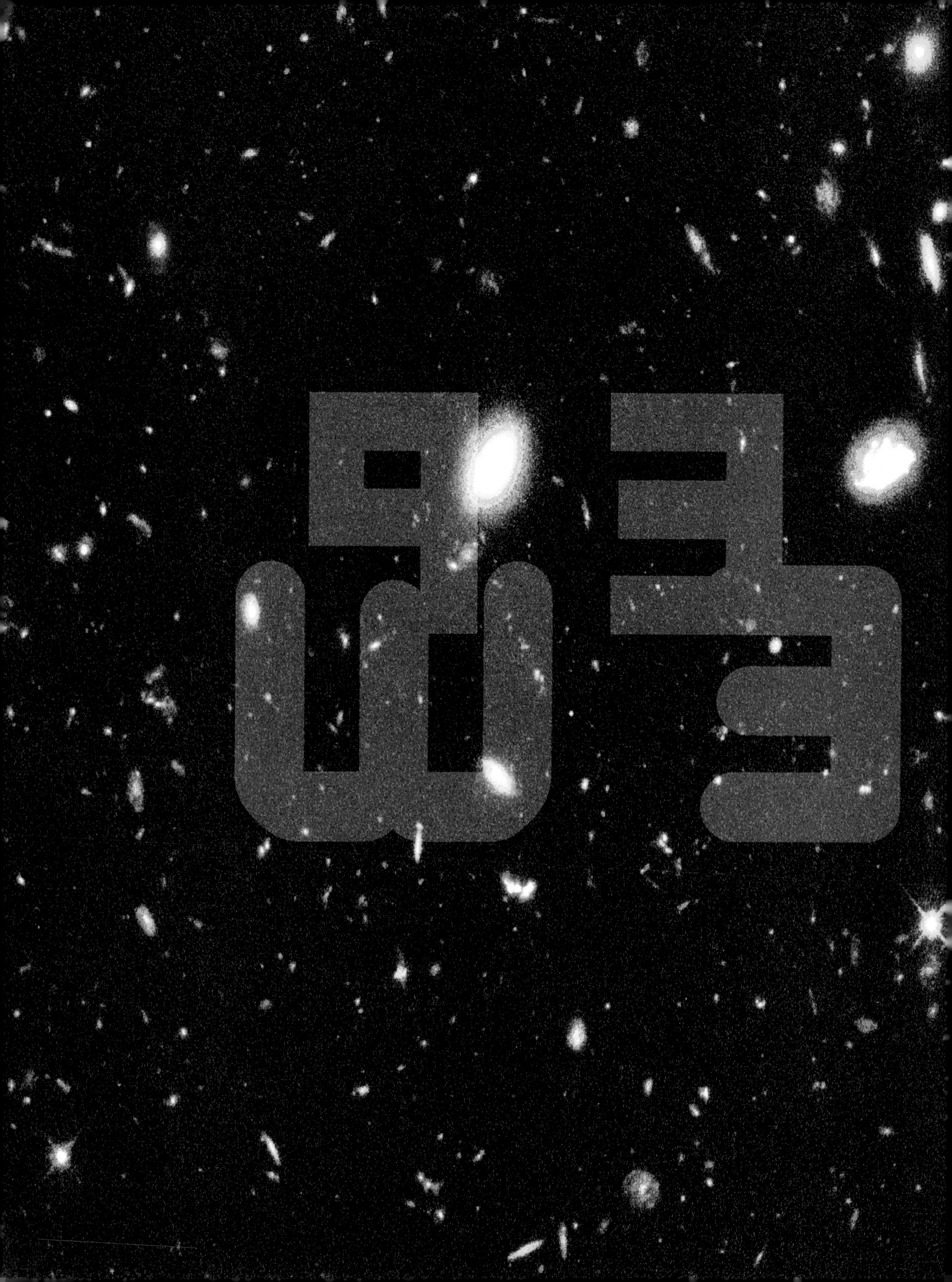

YOU WRITE THE LINKS BETWEEN
THE CORPSE AND THE UNIVERSE,
THE SWIMMING POOL AND THE TYPEFACE,
THE BRAIN AND THE BUTT,
THE BLESSED AND THE MEEK,
THE DATES OF BIRTH AND THE INTIMATIONS
THAT GO BEFORE DEATH,
THE DUST BEHIND WHEREISHERE.

OBSESSION
MEANS   DEMATERIAL
AUDIENCE

INSIDE FRONT AND BACK FLAPS SWEATY LETTERFORM [3D RENDER BY JAMES GLADMAN] PAGE 1 CORPSE FROM DALLAS, TEXAS CORONER'S OFFICE.

4-5 LIBBY **CLARKE**
ROBOT AND CHILD. VIDEO STILL FROM A SERIES CALLED "SICK OF BEING SEEN". **OBSESSION** I HAVE ALWAYS BEEN FASCINATED BY THE REFRAMING OF EXPERIENCE. **MEANS** VARIOUS TECHNIQUES OF PRINTING: BLOSSOMING OUT ON TO THE WEB, ON TO SCREENS, AND ON TO MYSELF IN THE FORM OF SCRIPT AND COSTUME. **MATERIAL/DEMATERIAL** AT FIRST I USED APPROPRIATION AND COLLAGE IN ORDER TO TRY AND DISRUPT THINGS ON PAPER. I REALIZE NOW THAT I NEED TO GET INTO THE RING MYSELF, AS A PERFORMER. I AM VEERING TOWARDS VIDEO AND FILM, DEVELOPING UNSETTLING SITUATIONS, DOCUMENTING THEM AND THEN USING THEM AS A BASE FOR FURTHER WORK. **AUDIENCE** THE AUDIENCE OF THE STAGED EVENT; THE AUDIENCE OF THE VIDEO [FELLOW ART STUDENTS]; FINALLY THE AUDIENCE OF THE PRINTED PIECE.
LIBBY CLARKE WAS BORN IN 1971 IN COVINGTON, VIRGINIA. SHE IS A FINE-ART PRINTMAKER, AND A RECENT CONVERT TO GRAPHIC DESIGN THROUGH GRADUATE STUDIES AT THE CRANBROOK ACADEMY OF ART.

PHOTOGRAPHS COURTESY OF PHOTODISC ON PAGES 22-23, 36-37, 50, 67, 106-107, 112-113, 120-121, 156-157 AND 192.

PHOTOGRAPHY BY LAURA HEYMAN FOR WHEREISHERE ON PAGES 38, 39, 82, 108, 144, 155, 152, 153, 164-165, 168-169, 174-175 + 177.

FONTS FOR **WHEREISHERE**: "DETROIT" DESIGNED BY OPTIMO AND "HUD" DESIGNED BY WORDS AND PICTURES FOR BUSINESS AND CULTURE.

8 JEFF **CASHDOLLAR**
SOMETHING ABOUT UNCERTAINTY. IMAGE OF THE OLYMPIC GAME "CURLING" FROM A VIDEO PROJECT USING SAMPLES FROM TELEVISION AND FILM. "HEISENBERG'S UNCERTAINTY PRINCIPLE STATES THAT A MEASUREMENT IS ONLY THE RESULT OF THE INTERACTION BETWEEN THE MEASURER AND THE MEASURED. MY WORK IS AN EXPLORATION OF THAT RELATIONSHIP. **OBSESSION** THE SPACE BEFORE THE ALPHA STATE. **MEANS** LO-FI STOLEN VIDEO **MATERIAL/DEMATERIAL** PRIMARILY DEMATERIAL **AUDIENCE** I MAKE THINGS FOR FRIENDS THAT I DON'T SEE ANYMORE.
JEFF CASHDOLLAR WAS BORN IN MORGANTOWN, WEST VIRGINIA IN 1965. EXPERIMENTING WITH FILM, TYPOGRAPHY AND DESIGN, HE RECEIVED HIS UNDERGRADUATE DEGREE IN FILM FROM NEW YORK UNIVERSITY, AND A MASTER OF FINE ARTS IN 2-D DESIGN FROM CRANBROOK ACADEMY OF ART. HE IS CURRENTLY WORKING FOR THE MAN.

9 SOURCE UNKNOWN.
12 CHILD DRAWING ON GREIMAN POSTER [PHOTO BY P. SCOTT MAKELA].
13 IMAGE OF LAMPREY FROM MICHIGAN DEPT. OF FISHERIES WEBSITE.
17 IMAGE OF LAURIE HAYCOCK MAKELA'S BRAIN HEMORRHAGE, CORNELL UNIVERSITY HOSPITAL, NEW YORK.
19 SOURCE UNKNOWN.

20-21 GREIMANSKI LABS

PHOTOGRAPHS OF THE VIEW FROM MIRACLE MANOR, A SPA BUILT IN 1948 ON MIRACLE HILL, OVERLOOKING THE DESERT WITH VIEWS OF MOUNT SAN JACINTO [PICTURED IN THE IMAGE]. A TWO-HOUR DRIVE FROM LOS ANGELES, THE SPA HAS ITS OWN WELL WATER THAT COMES OUT OF THE GROUND AT 158 DEGREES FAHRENHEIT. MIRACLE MANOR IS A COLLABORATIVE PROJECT BY APRIL GREIMAN AND MICHAEL ROTONDI. **ʀᴏᴄᴄᴇᴄᴄɪᴏɴᴄ** PEACE OF MIND. **ᴍᴇᴏᴜᴄ** AIR AND WATER.

APRIL GREIMAN WAS BORN IN NEW YORK. SHE STUDIED GRAPHIC DESIGN AT THE KANSAS CITY ART INSTITUTE, AND THE ALLGEMEINE KUNSTGEWERBESCHULE IN BASLE, SWITZERLAND, THEN MOVED TO LOS ANGELES IN 1976. GREIMAN HAS PARTICIPATED IN MUSEUM SHOWS IN THE USA, JAPAN, EUROPE AND ISRAEL. IN 1994 HER WORK WAS MOUNTED FOR A ONE-WOMAN SHOW IN BORDEAUX, FRANCE. SHE HAS IN THE PAST BEEN DIRECTOR OF THE VISUAL COMMUNICATIONS PROGRAM AT CALIFORNIA INSTITUTE OF THE ARTS. SHE IS AN INSTRUCTOR AT THE SOUTHERN CALIFORNIA INSTITUTE OF ARCHITECTURE.

MICHAEL ROTONDI IS A PRINCIPAL OF ROTO ARCHITECTS [FOUNDED IN 1991], AND IS ALSO A FACULTY MEMBER OF THE BOARD OF DIRECTORS OF SCI-ARC [SOUTHERN CALIFORNIA INSTITUTE OF ARCHITECTURE]. HE WAS ONE OF FIFTY PEOPLE WHO FOUNDED THE INSTITUTE IN 1972. IN 1976 HE FORMED MORPHOSIS WHICH CONTINUED UNTIL 1991. HE WAS THE CO-RECIPIENT OF THE AMERICAN ACADEMY AND INSTITUTE OF ARTS AND LETTERS AWARD IN ARCHITECTURE 1992. IN 1997 HE WAS SELECTED TO THE AMERICAN INSTITUTE OF ARCHITECTS COLLEGE OF FELLOWS FOR HIS CONTRIBUTIONS TO DESIGN AND EDUCATION.

22-23 AUSTRIA

24-27 STEFAN SAGMEISTER

24-25 **ARTIST'S TESTICLES AND BACK** WITH THE TITLE OF THIS BOOK GOUGED INTO HIS SKIN [PHOTOGRAPHS BY TOM SCHIERLITZ]. 26-27 **ARTIST'S OPINION** [ILLUSTRATED BY KEVIN MURPHY]. **ʀᴏᴄᴄᴇᴄᴄɪᴏɴᴄ** CALVIN KLEIN, AND HOW TO REALLY TOUCH SOMEBODY WITH SOMETHING PRINTED. **ᴍᴇᴏᴜᴄ** TO LIVE IN NEW YORK AMONG PEOPLE WHO ACTUALLY DO SOMETHING [AS OPPOSED TO VIENNA WHERE THEY TALK ABOUT DOING SOMETHING]. **ᴍᴏᴛᴇᴏɪᴏɪᴄ** PENCIL AND SKETCHBOOK; EVER SINCE ART SCHOOL I HAVE KEPT FAIRLY ORDERLY SKETCHBOOKS. I OFTEN GO BACK AND LOOK FOR IDEAS I COULDN'T USE AT THE TIME. **ᴏᴇᴍᴏᴛᴇᴏɪᴏɪᴄ** PHOTOSHOP, ILLUSTRATOR, QUARKXPRESS – I NEVER USE THEM. OUR LOVELY DESIGNER HJALTI KARLSSON DOES A LOT THOUGH. **ᴏᴜᴛɪᴇɴᴄᴇ** MY AUDIENCE CHANGES FROM PROJECT TO PROJECT: WE OBVIOUSLY TALK TO DIFFERENT GROUPS OF PEOPLE WHEN DESIGNING THE ROLLING STONES CD AND WHEN WE WORK ON A JAPANESE CALLIGRAPHY BOOK.

STEFAN SAGMEISTER WAS BORN AND EDUCATED IN AUSTRIA. HE RECEIVED HIS MASTER OF FINE ARTS DEGREE IN GRAPHIC DESIGN FROM THE UNIVERSITY OF APPLIED ARTS IN VIENNA, AND WENT ON TO ACQUIRE A MASTERS DEGREE FROM THE PRATT INSTITUTE IN NEW YORK. HE WAS CREATIVE DIRECTOR AT THE HONG KONG OFFICE OF ADVERTISING AGENCY LEO BURNETT, AND ALSO WORKED AT M&CO IN NEW YORK BEFORE FORMING SAGMEISTER INC. IN 1993. SPECIALIZING IN CD PACKAGING, SAGMEISTER HAS WORKED WITH THE ROLLING STONES, DAVID BYRNE, AEROSMITH AND PAT METHENY, AND HAS RECEIVED GRAMMY AWARD NOMINATIONS FOR PACKAGING FOR HP ZINKER, MARSHALL CRENSHAW AND LOU REED.

28-29 BRAZIL

[LEFT] STILL FROM *BUTT ROW* BY EVIL ANGEL FILMS. [RIGHT] PHOTOGRAPH OF RIO DE JANEIRO BY P. SCOTT MAKELA.

30-31 GRINGO CARDIA

TWO SET DESIGNS 30 **JULIETA DE FREUD** 31 **FICA COMIGO ESTA NOITE.** **ʀᴏᴄᴄᴇᴄᴄɪᴏɴᴄ** TO BRING VALUE TO THE UGLY, THE UNDERESTIMATED, THE POOR, THE MINORITIES AND TO THE TRADITIONAL URBAN CULTURE. TO UNDERMINE ALL FORMS OF PREJUDICE AND RACISM. TO DE-MYSTIFY ART AND TECHNIQUE AND BRING IT TO EVERYDAY LIFE SO THAT PEOPLE CAN REALIZE THAT ART IS EVERYWHERE AND ALL IT TAKES IS TO LOOK IN A DIFFERENT WAY. **ᴍᴇᴏᴜᴄ** APPLE MAC WITH PHOTOSHOP AND QUARKXPRESS, A BIG LIBRARY OF BOOKS AND MAGAZINES, TRAVELLING AROUND THE WORLD AND LEARNING FROM DIFFERENT CULTURES THEIR OWN WAYS OF LOOKING AND REPRESENTATION. **ᴏᴜᴛɪᴇɴᴄᴇ** YOUNG PEOPLE [RESTLESS AND WILLING TO BREAK THROUGH BARRIERS]. ARTISTS AND MUSICIANS, GAYS, MINORITIES [ETHNIC AND ARTISTIC], PEOPLE WHO WOULD RATHER PURSUE NEW THINGS INSTEAD OF THE TRADITIONAL AND CONSERVATIVE.

GRINGO CARDIA IS A GRAPHIC DESIGNER, SET DESIGNER, ARCHITECT, ART DIRECTOR AND DIRECTOR OF MUSIC VIDEOS. BORN IN BRAZIL IN 1957, HE STUDIED ARCHITECTURE AT THE UFRG IN RIO DE JANEIRO. AWARDS RECEIVED BY CARDIA INCLUDE AN MTV MUSIC AWARD IN 1990 AND A BRASILIA CINEMA FESTIVAL AWARD FOR ART DIRECTING THE FILM *LILI CARABINA*.

32-33 BELORUSSIA

BELORUS BRIDES. <WWW.BELARUS.NET/PEOPLE/LADY/INDEX.HTM>

34-35 ALEXEI TYLEVICH

34 **WITHOUT YOU I AM NOTHING.** "THE EROTICIZED STATE OF SENSORY DEPRIVATION, WHICH IN ITSELF IS PERVERSE. FACTUAL DREAMS TRANSFORMED INTO DEMONIC HALLUCINATIONS. THE GREY AREA BETWEEN THE REPULSIVE AND THE ATTRACTIVE WHERE THOSE DEFINITIONS BECOME INTERCHANGEABLE." CREATED FOR *WHEREISHERE*.

35 STILL FROM ONE OF A SERIES OF COMMERCIALS FOR **NIKE SOCCER**. CREATED FOR ADVERTISING AGENCY WIEDEN & KENNEDY, PORTLAND. THE CAMPAIGN WAS FOR MEXICO AND CHILE, AND EACH AD WAS BASED ON ONE OF THE SEVEN DEADLY SINS. CREATED BY TYLEVICH WITH ART DIRECTION BY ARTY TAN AND COPYWRITING BY MATT ELHARDT. **ʀᴏᴄᴄᴇᴄᴄɪᴏɴᴄ** THE ABILITY OF IMAGES TO ELICIT A PHYSICAL RESPONSE IN THE BODY. I GET BORED QUITE EASILY AND DEVELOP NEW OBSESSIONS ON A DAILY BASIS. **ᴍᴇᴏᴜᴄ** FEEDING THE MONSTER. THE WORK PROCESS IS QUITE ORDINARY; FROM ANALOGUE TO DIGITAL AND BACK. THE PROCESS IS OF NO GREAT IMPORTANCE AS LONG AS THE ORIGINAL INTENT REMAINS CLEAR. **ᴍᴏᴛᴇᴏɪᴏɪᴄ/ᴏᴇᴍᴏᴛᴇᴏɪᴏɪᴄ** ANYTHING GOES, AND THEN IT GETS SCANNED IN. I PREFER LO-FI THINGS WITH A TOUCH OF THE SUBLIME. SECOND-HAND, MARGINAL AND UNSTABLE MAKE UP FOR THE EXOTIC. THE SOURCES OF INSPIRATION FLUCTUATE RAPIDLY IN THE COURSE OF ONE DAY. VISUAL TURN-ONS ARE EVERYWHERE YOU LOOK. WATCHING NETWORK TELEVISION MAKES ME ILL. **ᴏᴜᴛɪᴇɴᴄᴇ** BORED AND APATHETIC. WAITING FOR SOMETHING TO HAPPEN. THE ULTIMATE JUDGE OF WHAT IS RELEVANT.

ALEXEI TYLEVICH WAS BORN IN MINSK, BELARUS IN 1972. HE STUDIED PAINTING FOR THREE YEARS BEFORE EMIGRATING TO THE USA IN 1989, GRADUATING WITH A BACHELOR OF FINE ARTS DEGREE FROM THE MINNEAPOLIS COLLEGE OF ART AND DESIGN IN 1994. TYLEVICH SPECIALIZES IN ART DIRECTION FOR TELEVISION AND COMMERCIALS, COMPUTER ANIMATION AND MOTION GRAPHICS, DESIGN FOR PRINT AND TYPEFACE DESIGN. HIS CLIENTS INCLUDE MGM, SEGA, NIKE AND DKNY. FOR THREE YEARS TYLEVICH SERVED AS ART DIRECTOR AT CHANNEL ONE NEWS IN LOS ANGELES, A TELEVISION STATION THAT BROADCASTS DAILY NEWS TO 8.5 MILLION HIGH-SCHOOL STUDENTS. HE THEN SET UP HIS OWN DESIGN STUDIO. THE RECIPIENT OF NUMEROUS AWARDS, HE ALSO LECTURES INTERNATIONALLY.

36-37 CANADA

38-39 IAN PHILLIPS

38 **SNACKS.** MAIL-ART PROJECT CONTAINING EXAMPLES OF LOST PET POSTERS FOUND IN NEIGHBOURHOODS AROUND THE WORLD.

39 **QUINCEAÑERA.** A BOOK CONTAINING 15 LUST-FILLED POEMS, WRITTEN BY ELISSA JOY AND DESIGNED BY PAS DE CHANCE. DECORATED WITH ILLUSTRATIONS OF COLUMBINE AND HARLEQUIN, THE COVER IS HAND PRINTED ON JAPANESE WOOD PAPER. 3D PEEK-A-BOO EYEBALLS STARE UP AS THE READER TURNS THE PAGES. EACH COPY OF THE BOOK HAS A HAND-MADE DRESS ON THE COVER. **ʀᴏᴄᴄᴇᴄᴄɪᴏɴᴄ** I'M CONSTANTLY COMING UP WITH NEW IDEAS FOR BOOKS; I ALSO BECOME OBSESSED WITH DIFFERENT KINDS OF IMAGES – FIRST IT WAS MISSING PET POSTERS, THEN IT WAS CANDY BOXES, THEN IT WAS ARTWORK ON CARDBOARD BOXES FROM THE GROCERY STORE. MY CURRENT IMAGE OBSESSION IS OLD, HAND-PAINTED STORE SIGNAGE WHICH IS RAPIDLY DISAPPEARING FROM TORONTO. **ᴍᴇᴏᴜᴄ** I WORK AS A FREELANCE ILLUSTRATOR WHICH GIVES ME A GREAT DEAL OF CONTROL OVER MY OWN TIME. IN THE BOOKS I AM ABLE TO EXPERIMENT – THE BOOKS DON'T LOOK ANYTHING LIKE THE COMMERCIAL ART I DO. SEEMS THAT IT IS ALL REALLY ABOUT TIME AND MONEY. **ᴍᴏᴛᴇᴏɪᴏɪᴄ/ᴏᴇᴍᴏᴛᴇᴏɪᴏɪᴄ** ANYTHING I CAN FIND IN FLAT MULTIPLES FOR AS LITTLE MONEY AS POSSIBLE. I HAVE BOXES OF JUNK THAT I HOPE TO UTILIZE IN SOME PROJECT. I COLLECT MATERIALS THROUGH THE MAIL-ART NETWORK. I'VE BEEN COLLECTING SCRAPS OF PAPER FROM GARBAGE OVER THE YEARS. **ᴏᴜᴛɪᴇɴᴄᴇ** I GET LETTERS FROM ALL KINDS OF PEOPLE. IN THE LAST YEAR OR TWO THE VOLUME OF MAIL HAS INCREASED TO A POINT WHERE I CAN'T DO ANYTHING EXCEPT DEAL WITH THE ORDERS, SO ONCE A MONTH I BIND ALL THE MAIL INTO BOOK FORMAT AND RUBBER STAMP THE DATE ON THE FRONT COVER AND STICK IT ON A SHELF. I HAVE 24 OR 25 VOLUMES FROM THE LAST YEAR ALONE.

TORONTO-BASED FREELANCE ILLUSTRATOR IAN PHILLIPS BEGAN PUBLISHING SMALL PERSONAL BOOKS FUSING ILLUSTRATION, COMICS, FOUND AND ORIGINAL TEXT IN 1986 UNDER THE BANNER MAGA PUBLICATIONS [NOW PAS DE CHANCE]. IN 1993 PAS DE CHANCE BEGAN MAILING LITTLE BOOKLETS TO MAIL-ARTISTS ALL OVER THE WORLD. EACH MAIL-ARTIST ADDS SOMETHING OF THEIR OWN AND SENDS THE BOOK TO ANOTHER ARTIST. WHEN THE BOOK IS FULL IT IS RETURNED TO PAS DE CHANCE FOR PUBLIC DISPLAY.

40-41 44 Bruce MAU

40-41 DETAIL FROM THE INNER COVER OF THE LIBERTINE READER: EROTICISM AND ENLIGHTENMENT IN EIGHTEENTH-CENTURY FRANCE. ABOUNDING WITH SEX, PASSION AND THE ABUSE OF POWER IN THE ROYAL COURTS OF FRANCE, THE COVER IS FROM TWO PAINTINGS BY FRAGONARD: THE FURTIVE KISS AND THE BOLT. A REMOVABLE TRANSLUCENT DUST JACKET CONCEALS WHAT IS BEING READ AND IS A FURTHER PLAY ON DRESSING, UNDRESSING AND SEDUCTION. 44 POSTER PROMOTING THE SCHOOL OF ARCHITECTURE PROGRAMME AT RICE UNIVERSITY, WHOSE PURPOSE IS TO PUSH THE EXPECTATION OF WHAT AN ARCHITECTURE PROGRAMME CAN OFFER. BY BRUCE MAU WITH YOSHI WATERHOUSE AND BRANDON HOOKWAY.

BRUCE MAU DESIGN [BMD] WAS FOUNDED IN 1985. IT HAS LONG-TERM CREATIVE PARTNERSHIPS WITH ORGANIZATIONS SUCH AS THE GETTY RESEARCH INSTITUTE, LOS ANGELES, AND ZONE BOOKS, NEW YORK, WITH SPECIFIC COMMISSIONS FROM THE ANDY WARHOL MUSEUM, THE NETHERLANDS ARCHITECTURE INSTITUTE AND THE ART GALLERY OF ONTARIO. INTERNATIONAL CLIENTS INCLUDE SWATCH, PHAIDON PRESS AND SONY CLASSICAL. BRUCE MAU WAS BORN IN CANADA IN 1960, AND STUDIED AT THE ONTARIO COLLEGE OF ART. HE WORKED AT PENTAGRAM UK BEFORE RETURNING TO CANADA TO SET UP BRUCE MAU DESIGN. HIS WORK HAS BEEN FEATURED IN MAJOR INTERNATIONAL PUBLICATIONS AND HAS RECEIVED NUMEROUS AWARDS. HE HAS ENGAGED IN COLLABORATIVE PARTNERSHIPS WITH ARCHITECTS, ARTISTS AND WRITERS INCLUDING CLAES OLDENBURG, AND REM KOOLHAAS WITH WHOM HE COLLABORATED ON S,M,L,XL.

45 Derek BARNETT

INTERFACE. AN INTERACTIVE, SELF-INITIATED CD-ROM PROJECT WHICH EXPLORES THE BODY AS LANDSCAPE. PHOTOGRAPHY FOR INTERFACE BY SHELLE GUHLE. OBSESSIONS ABSTRACT NARRATIVES, DIALECTIC, STATISTICS, CONTEMPORARY ART PRACTICES, ALIENATION, MEMORY, SYSTEMS, IDEOLOGIES, DIASPORA, DICHOTOMY AND LISTS. MEANS E-MAIL HAS OPENED A FEW INTERNATIONAL DOORS, BUT I WISH I OWNED A FAX MACHINE. MATERIALS/IMMATERIALS SUBVERSION WITHIN THE DESIGN HELPS TO CONTEXTUALIZE THE WORK ON MORE LEVELS OF INTERPRETATION. THIS ALLOWANCE OF CONFLICTING "MYSTERIES" GIVES A DIALECTIC THAT HOPEFULLY COMMUNICATES A PLURALITY. AUDIENCE I AM INTERESTED IN MANY AUDIENCES. COMMUNICATION IS A PROCESS OF LAYERING MEANING – REFERENTIAL, EXPLICIT, IMPLICIT AND SYMPTOMATIC. ALL ARE SIGNIFICANT AND ALL ARE INTERESTING TO DIFFERENT AUDIENCES. DESIGN IS A TEMPORAL ARTIFICE OF THE NOW. DESIGNERS ARE SIMPLY DOCUMENTORS OF A WORLD THAT IS BIGGER THAN THEY ARE.

DEREK BARNETT WAS BORN IN REGINA, SASKATCHEWAN, CANADA IN 1971. HE WORKS IN COLLABORATION WITH SHELLE GUHLE IN VANCOUVER, CANADA UNDER THE NAME FOF, AN ACRONYM THAT LACKS A STATIC IDENTITY. BARNETT AND GUHLE PREFER TO KEEP THEIR AIMS AMBIGUOUS; THEY WORK BOTH AS ARTISTS AND DESIGNERS, OFTEN ON PROJECTS WHICH OFFER NO FINANCIAL REWARD. THEIR NEXT PROJECT IS A DIGITAL ZINE WHICH WILL BE ENTITLED PHYLE.

46-49 Floria SIGISMONDI

46 MARILYN MANSON MUSIC VIDEO BEAUTIFUL PEOPLE. THE MOUTHPIECE WAS USED AS A SYMBOL TO SHOW HOW GOVERNMENTS RESTRAIN THE MASSES THROUGH PHYSICAL AND MENTAL DEVICES. 47 LUPUS DISEASE. IN THIS COMMERCIAL, A WOMAN STRUGGLES TO GET OUT OF A GLASS BOX. SHE CRIES OUT BUT NO ONE HEARS HER; AT THE SAME TIME THE BOX IS GETTING SMALLER. 48-49 TRICKY MUSIC VIDEO SHE MAKES ME WANNA DIE. OBSESSIONS DECONSTRUCTION OF THE HUMAN BODY; I COLLECT DOLLS AND OTHER OBJECTS THAT REPRESENT HUMANS. I FEEL LIKE A MODERN-DAY DR FRANKENSTEIN. WATER SEEMS TO BE A RECURRING THEME – MY IDEAS WAVER ON THE EDGE OF TWO EXTREMES, BLACK OR WHITE, GOOD OR EVIL [THE POLAR OPPOSITES]. MEANS ISOLATION FROM FAMILY, FRIENDS, PHONE AND FAX. ABSOLUTE QUIET. SLEEP DEPRIVATION HELPS THE PROCESS – IT OPENS THE SUBCONSCIOUS, THE MOMENT BETWEEN CONSCIOUSNESS AND DEEP SLEEP [USUALLY FOR ME BETWEEN 4.00 AND 5.00 IN THE MORNING]; FOR THAT MOMENT PRIOR TO WAKING UP I KEEP A NOTEBOOK BY THE BED TO DOCUMENT IDEAS. MATERIALS/IMMATERIALS HUMAN REPRESENTATIONS – FOR EXAMPLE DOLLS, WOODEN HANDS, FEET, HEADS, DRESSMAKING DOLLS – I LOVE SCULPTURES WITH THESE OBJECTS. VISUAL STIMULI INCLUDE ART GALLERIES, FILMS AND ART BOOKS, PLUS MUSIC [A MUST]. AUDIENCE I DON'T THINK OF MY AUDIENCE WHEN I'M WORKING. I THINK OF MY IDEAS AND IMAGES AS THERAPY THROUGH ART.

FLORIA SIGISMONDI WAS BORN IN 1965 IN PESCARA, ITALY, AND EMIGRATED TO ONTARIO, CANADA WITH HER FAMILY IN 1967. IN 1987 SHE STUDIED AT THE ONTARIO COLLEGE OF ART, LEAVING TO PURSUE A CAREER AS A FASHION PHOTOGRAPHER. SHE HAS CREATED VIDEOS FOR MUSIC ARTISTS INCLUDING DAVID BOWIE, MARILYN MANSON AND TRICKY. SHE ALSO DIRECTS COMMERCIALS FOR CLIENTS INCLUDING COCA-COLA AND ADIDAS.

FRANCE

50-51 [RIGHT] DETAIL OF A CORRODED ARTERY FROM THE UNIVERSITY OF MICHIGAN PHOTO-LIBRARY.

52-53 Pierre DISCIULLO

52 ENTRANCE SIGNAGE FOR THE UNIVERSITY OF MEDICINE OF BOBIGNY, NEAR PARIS. SANTÉ MEANS "HEALTH"; THE TYPEFACE FOR THE SIGNAGE IS MINIMUM BICHRO. PHOTOGRAPH BY PASCAL HOUDART. 53 CHOOSE YOUR AMNESIA, A POSTER ABOUT THE CIVIL WAR IN ALGERIA, WHERE APPROXIMATELY 60,000 PEOPLE HAVE DIED IN THE CONFLICT OVER THE PAST SIX YEARS. OBSESSIONS TO WIN MORE TIME AND SPACE TO WORK ON MY EXPERIENCES. I ENJOY MY JOB AS A GRAPHIC DESIGNER, BUT BECOME NERVOUS AND UNHAPPY AFTER THREE WEEKS OF NOT WORKING ON MY RESEARCH. MEANS I LIKE TO DISCOVER A LOT OF PEOPLE AND SOCIAL SITUATIONS AND TO PARTICIPATE WITH MY SMALL POSSIBILITIES OF DESIGN. MATERIALS/IMMATERIALS EACH TIME OF COURSE FOR A SPECIFIC OBJECT A SPECIFIC AUDIENCE, AND A DIFFERENT MATERIAL TO JOIN THIS AUDIENCE. AUDIENCE MY GREAT PLEASURE IS TO ALTERNATE FROM ONE AUDIENCE TO ANOTHER, FROM THE PEOPLE WALKING ON THE STREET TO THE VERY SPECIFIC AUDIENCE [AND EACH TIME DIFFERENT] OF MY PERSONAL PUBLICATION QUI? RÉSISTE. DESIGNING A TYPEFACE FOR A WHOLE COMMUNITY [TARGI PEOPLE] OFFERS AN AUDIENCE OF POTENTIALLY SIX MILLION.

PIERRE DI SCIULLO WAS BORN IN 1962 IN PARIS WHERE HE CONTINUES TO LIVE AND WORK. SINCE 1983 HE HAS SELF-PUBLISHED THE JOURNAL QUI? RÉSISTE – EACH ISSUE EXPLORES THEMES SUCH AS SEDUCTION AND TRUTH. HE PREFERS "STRANGE PROJECTS" AND SPECIALIZES IN TYPEFACE DESIGN. PROJECTS INCLUDE QUANTANGE, A PHONETICALLY BASED FONT WHICH SPELLS OUT THE SOUNDS OF THE FRENCH LANGUAGE, AND BASNODA, A FONT DESIGNED FOR VERTICAL PALINDROMIC TEXTS. HE HAS DESIGNED FIVE FONTS FOR ELECTRONIC PUBLISHING IN THE TIFINAGH WRITING SYSTEM FOR THE TARGI PEOPLE OF THE SAHARA. IN 1995 HE WON THE CHARLES NYPELS AWARD IN THE NETHERLANDS.

GERMANY

54-55 FROM BERNER SCIENTIFIC MACHINE SHOP [STILLS BY P. SCOTT MAKELA].

56-57 surFACE

CD COVER FOR THE BAND REKORD, PHOTOGRAPHY AND DESIGN BY MARKUS WEISBECK. OBSESSIONS SWIMMING AND CYCLING IN THE EARLY MORNING. MEANS GOOD MUSIC, OPEN EYES AND A FAST MACHINE. MATERIALS/IMMATERIALS THE RIGHT SOUNDTRACK. AUDIENCE EVERYDAY PEOPLE WITH THE RIGHT MIND.

MARKUS WEISBECK, THOMAS GLAUNINGER AND ANDREAS VITT WORKED IN A LOOSE NETWORK FOR APPROXIMATELY SIX YEARS BEFORE ESTABLISHING THE COMPANY SURFACE IN 1997. THEY COVER A NUMBER OF DISCIPLINES INCLUDING MULTIMEDIA, HUMAN INTERFACE DESIGN, PRINT GRAPHICS AND CLUB CORPORATE DESIGN. IN ADDITION, AS MUSIC FANS AND PART-TIME DJs THEY ARE ENTHUSIASTIC ABOUT NIGHTLIFE AND CLUB CULTURE.

58-60 Ali KEPENEK

58 THE PHOTOGRAPHER'S FIRST APARTMENT. 60 FROM AN EXHIBITION AND BOOK ABOUT EROTIC PHOTOGRAPHY. 59 PHOTOGRAPH FROM PERSONAL PHOTOGRAPHIC DIARY. OBSESSIONS ALL I WANT TO DO IS TAKE PICTURES THAT MIGHT MEAN SOMETHING TO PEOPLE. PRIVATE OBSESSIONS: I TAKE LOADS OF PICTURES OF MY BOYFRIEND. I'M KIND OF OBSESSED BY HIM AND CONTINUE TRYING TO GET TO HIS CORE. I'VE STARTED TAKING SELF-PORTRAITS. WHEN I'M IN A HOTEL ROOM ON MY OWN I TAKE PICTURES OF MYSELF NAKED. MEANS I DON'T DIFFER BETWEEN PICTURES FOR EXHIBITIONS AND COMMISSIONED WORK. IN THE END I ALWAYS TAKE THE PICTURE FOR MYSELF. I HAVE TO LIKE THE PICTURES. MATERIALS/IMMATERIALS I NEED DAYLIGHT AND A CAMERA. THAT'S ALL. I'M NOT INTERESTED IN THE LATEST TECHNONOLGY. IN THAT SENSE I'M A CLASSIC PHOTOGRAPHER.

ALI KEPENEK WAS BORN IN SIVAS, TURKEY IN 1968. SINCE 1972 HE HAS LIVED IN GERMANY, ATTENDING SCHOOLS IN COLOGNE AND BERLIN. FROM 1989 TO 1991 HE ATTENDED THE LETTE PHOTOGRAPHIC SCHOOL AND HAS BEEN A FULL TIME PHOTOGRAPHER EVER SINCE. HE HAS REGULAR SOLO EXHIBITIONS, INCLUDING "HOMAGE TO WOMAN" AT THE GALERIE NEU IN BERLIN IN 1994, PLUS SEVERAL EXHIBITIONS AT GALERIE WOLF IN BERLIN. GROUP EXHIBITIONS HAVE INCLUDED THE AUSTRIAN TRIENNALE FOR PHOTOGRAPHY. HE WORKS REGULARLY FOR MARIE CLAIRE, VOGUE AND K7.

61 Gerhard VORMWALD

PHOTOGRAPH ENTITLED CHINESE FOOD 2 FROM A SERIES CALLED MONUMENT OF FOODSTUFFS AND SEMI-LUXURIES. OBSESSIONS I AM OBSESSED BY EVERYTHING CONCERNING FOODSTUFFS AND SEMI-LUXURIES. MATERIALS/IMMATERIALS I WORK WITH CLASSICAL AS WELL AS DIGITAL PHOTOGRAPHIC MEDIUMS. AUDIENCE I DO IT FOR

MYSELF, AND THEN FOR MY GALLERIES, FOR THE PUBLIC TO SEE.
GERHARD VORMWALD WAS BORN IN HEIDELBERG, GERMANY IN 1948. BETWEEN 1966 AND 1971 HE STUDIED AT THE APPLIED ARTS SCHOOL IN MANNHEIM. IN 1970, WITH NO FORMAL TRAINING IN PHOTOGRAPHY, HE BEGAN WORKING AS A STAGE PHOTOGRAPHER FOR THE NATIONAL THEATRE IN MANNHEIM. EMIGRATING TO PARIS IN 1983 HE CONTINUED TO WORK WITH ADVERTISING AND EDITORIAL PHOTOGRAPHY. SINCE 1990 HE HAS DEVOTED AN INCREASING AMOUNT OF TIME TO HIS PERSONAL PORTFOLIO. HE LECTURES AND EXHIBITS INTERNATIONALLY. HIS WORK HAS APPEARED IN THE MAGAZINES *TIME* AND *STERN*.

64-65 HENRYK **WEIFFENBACH**

TWO PHOTOGRAPHS FROM THE BERLIN ART PERFORMANCE GROUP "DEAD CHICKENS". 64 **KLEINE MUTTI** IS A PNEUMATICALLY OPERATED MACHINE USED AS A CHARACTER IN PERFORMANCES, BUILT BY H. HEINER. DEAD CHICKENS BUILD MACHINES, MAKE MONSTERS, PLAY MUSIC AND GIVE PERFORMANCES. THE GROUP IS MADE UP OF HANNES HEINER, KAI, BREEDE C.C., NILS PETERS, WERNER TRUNK AND HENRYK WEIFFENBACH. 65 **DEAD CHICKENS 1986.** KAI AND H. HEINER IN THE EARLY DAYS OF DEAD CHICKENS SURROUNDED BY THE STAGE ENVIRONMENT. THIS WAS THE FIRST OFFICIAL PICTURE OF DEAD CHICKENS. OBSESSIONS FAIRYTALE PHOTOGRAPHS. MEANS I GO TO PLACES AND SEE WHAT'S UP, SOMETIMES TO MY STUDIO. MATERIALS/DE-MATERIALS 36MM-6X6CM, COLOUR/BLACK AND WHITE. AUDIENCE PEOPLE LIKE US.
HENRYK WEIFFENBACH WAS BORN IN WEST BERLIN IN 1965. SINCE 1986 HE HAS WORKED WITH THE BERLIN UNDERGROUND ART AND PERFORMANCE GROUP DEAD CHICKENS. FROM 1985 TO 1989 HE WORKED IN AMSTERDAM AND BERLIN, ASSISTING PHOTO AND TELEVISION JOURNALISTS AND STUDIO PHOTOGRAPHERS. HE ALSO PARTICIPATED IN SEVERAL GROUP EXHIBITIONS OF PHOTOGRAPHY AND ART IN BERLIN AND AMSTERDAM. IN 1990 HE FOUNDED THE DEAD CHICKENS WAREHOUSE GALLERY IN BERLIN. AFTER MOVING TO THE EASTERN PART OF BERLIN, WEIFFENBACH ORGANIZED FESTIVALS, EXHIBITIONS, ART CLUBS AND PERFORMANCE PROJECTS. HE IS A FOUNDING MEMBER AND ORGANIZER OF HAUS SCHWARZENBERG ART ASSOCIATION IN BERLIN.

66 HUNGARY
FROM THE BUDAPEST CD GUIDE TO ADULT ENTERTAINMENT.

68-69 ZSOLT **CZAKÓ**

DETAILS FROM TWO POSTERS. 68 **GO FURTHER** 69 **COME CLOSER** OBSESSIONS OBSESSION. MEANS COMMUNICATION IS MOST IMPORTANT, THEREFORE I ONLY WORK FOR THOSE CLIENTS WITH WHOM A POSITIVE, DIRECT COMMUNICATION CAN BE ACHIEVED. MONEY IS NOT AN ISSUE. MATERIALS/DE-MATERIALS PHOTOGRAPHY, COMPUTERS, PRINT. AUDIENCE I AM MY CLIENT AND AT THE SAME TIME I AM MYSELF TOO – THEREFORE MY WORK SHOULD PLEASE ME.
ZSOLT CZAKÓ WAS BORN IN 1965 IN PÉCS, HUNGARY. AFTER STUDYING AT THE HUNGARIAN ACADEMY OF APPLIED ART AND DESIGN, HE COMPLETED A SCHOLARSHIP OF THE CHICAGO ARTS INTERNATIONAL PROGRAM. SINCE THEN HE HAS WORKED IN BUDAPEST. HIS CLIENTS INCLUDE MTV [HUNGARIAN NATIONAL TELEVISION] AND CHANNELS 1 AND 2, FOR WHOM HE CREATED 22 SHORT FILMS BASED ON THE PAST 40 YEARS OF HUNGARIAN BROADCASTING, THE NUCLEAR POWER CENTRE PAKS, AND MATAVCOM, THE TELECOMMUNICATIONS COMPANY.

70-71 ITALY
MONK GIVING A TOUR OF AN ISLAND MONASTERY NEAR VENICE, ITALY, 1998 [PHOTOGRAPHED BY LAURIE HAYCOCK MAKELA].

72-73 KRI**SMA**

100 **UNCENSORED IMAGES.** A SELF-INITIATED VIDEO ART PROJECT USING UNCENSORED PROGRAMMING SCREENED ON SATELLITE TELEVISION OVER THE COURSE OF A WEEK. OBSESSIONS CELERY. MEANS BREATH. MATERIALS/DE-MATERIALS WATER: THE MINERAL THAT MOVES. AUDIENCE A NUMBER WITH FEELINGS.
KRISMA ARE MAURIZIO ARCIERI AND CRISTINA MOSER. ARCIERI BEGAN HIS CAREER AS A MUSICIAN IN 1965 IN A GROUP CALLED NEWDADA WHO TOURED WITH THE BEATLES AND THE WHO. FROM 1968 TO 1976 HE HAD A SOLO CAREER, RELEASING SEVEN ALBUMS. IN 1976 ARCIERI AND MOSER FOUNDED KRISMA, A GROUP SPECIALIZING IN ELECTRONIC MUSIC, COMPOSING, PRODUCTION AND VIDEO, WORKING ON PERSONAL PROJECTS AND WITH COMPANIES SUCH AS POLYDOR AND ATLANTIC RECORDS. SINCE 1982 THEY HAVE CONCENTRATED ON VIDEO AND PRODUCTION WORK, AND IN 1986 BEGAN WORKING FOR TELEVISION CHANNELS, NOTABLY FOR RAI, ITALY'S MAIN TELEVISION STATION. THEY HAVE CREATED MANY VIDEO ART PIECES AND INSTALLATIONS, AND HAVE WORKED WITH ART GROUPS SUCH AS FLUXUS. IN 1988 THEY JOINED FABRICA, WHERE THEY CONTINUE TO WORK.

74-75 NICOLA **SCHWARTZ**

TWO PHOTOGRAPHS. 74 **YOU ARE REALLY TRYING BUT I CAN'T GET CLOSER.** 75 **I FEEL NUMB BUT IT REALLY DOESN'T MATTER BECAUSE YOU CAN'T TELL.** OBSESSIONS I AM OBSESSED WITH CONTRADICTIONS, THE INSIDE BECOMES THE OUTSIDE, I DESIRE WET YET I FEEL DRY. I LIVE TO DIE AND THE IN-BETWEEN. MEANS LISTENING, SMELLING, TOUCHING AND WHAT I CAN'T DESCRIBE. MATERIALS/DE-MATERIALS OLIVE OIL, GARLIC, CHILLI PEPPER, TOMATO, SUGAR, SALT, PASTA AND FRESH BASIL AUDIENCE THAT SPECIAL PERSON I KEEP MISSING.
NICOLA SCHWARTZ WAS BORN IN ITALY IN 1970. HE MOVED TO AMERICA AND THEN BRITAIN WHERE HE ATTENDED THE ROYAL COLLEGE OF ART. HIS WORK HAS APPEARED IN PUBLICATIONS INCLUDING *SURFACE*, *DAZED & CONFUSED*, JAPANESE *ELLE*, *APERTURE NEW YORK*, AND *THE MAGIC SPONGE* [WITH VAUGHAN OLIVER].

76-77 ISRAEL
IMAGE ENTITLED "PUCKER UP" FROM THE SALONIKA REUNION GALLERY.

78-79 DEKEL **BOBROV**

PAGES FROM THE BOOK **THE SCRIPTWRITER AND REALITY,** A SHORT STORY BY ORLY CASTLE-BLOOM. 78 THE READER PASSES FROM A NARRATIVE SPHERE TO ANOTHER FORMED BY CINEMATIC FRAMING AND ICONS. 79 MATERIALS FROM TEL AVIV STREETS WERE USED, INCLUDING A MAP AND A PHOTOCOPY OF AN ISRAELI IDENTITY CARD. OBSESSIONS FOOD, BOOKS, NEWSPAPERS AND MAGAZINES. MEANS APPLE MAC, OPTIC SCANNER, TELEPHONE, FAX AND INTERNET. MATERIALS/DE-MATERIALS ANYTHING I FIND ON THE STREETS: RECEIPTS, SIGNS, NOTES, OLD PACKAGES AND SO ON. DE-MATERIALS: IMAGES STORED IN RESERVOIRS, IMAGES PROCESSED THROUGH PHOTOSHOP. AUDIENCE ANYONE WALKING ON THE STREET.
DEKEL BOBROV WAS BORN IN 1970 AT KINERET, A KIBBUTZ ON THE SHORES OF GALILEE. FROM 1988 TO 1991 HE DID MILITARY SERVICE AS A GRAPHIC DESIGNER FOR THE ISRAELI NAVY, THEN SPENT FOUR YEARS STUDYING DESIGN AT THE VITAL DESIGN CENTRE, TEL AVIV. HE HAS STAYED IN TEL AVIV SINCE, WORKING AT THE STUDIOS OF YORAM RUBINGER, MICHEL OPATOWSKY AND PHILIPPE BOULAKIA.

80-81 JAPAN
RANDOM SHOTS FROM JAPANESE TELEVISION BY P. SCOTT MAKELA.

82-83 HIRO **SUGIYAMA**

PAGES FROM TWO LIMITED-EDITION BOOKS. 82 **REVERSE SIDE NEW REALITY NEW PRINTINGS** 83 **APPEARANCES ARE OFTEN DECEPTIVE** OBSESSIONS PHOTOGRAPHY AND MAKING BOOKS. MATERIALS/DE-MATERIALS BRESIDIN [PAPER] AND ACRYLIC. AUDIENCE GOOD VIBRATIONS PEOPLE SYMPATHISE WITH ME.
HIRO SUGIYAMA WAS BORN IN 1962 IN TOKYO. SUGIYAMA GRADUATED FROM THE TOKYO ART SCHOOL IN 1987 AND WORKS FOR CLIENTS SUCH AS SONY, NISSAN AND SAMSUNG. WHEN NOT CONCENTRATING ON COMMISSIONED WORK, SUGIYAMA PRODUCES A SERIES OF LIMITED-EDITION ART BOOKS UNDER THE BANNER ENLIGHTENMENT PUBLISHING IN COLLABORATION WITH PRINTING COMPANY GRAPH CO. LTD. SUGIYAMA HAS ALSO PRODUCED A BOOK COLLABORATING WITH EIGHT OTHER ILLUSTRATORS, THE CONTENTS OF WHICH HAVE SINCE BEEN USED FOR AN EXHIBITION IN JAPAN.

84-85 TAKASHI **HOMMA**

PHOTOGRAPHS FROM THE BOOK **TOKYO TEENS.** 84 TYPICAL VIEW OF THE SUBURBS OF TOKYO. 85 BEDROOM OF A TEENAGE MALE DJ. OBSESSIONS RECORD EVERYTHING. MEANS I CAN DO AS I WANT OR TAKE A LOT OF MONEY. MATERIALS/DE-MATERIALS FAX MACHINE. AUDIENCE PEOPLE WHO CAN THINK BY FREEDOM.
TAKASHI HOMMA WAS BORN IN TOKYO IN 1962. AFTER STUDYING PHOTOGRAPHY AT NIHON UNIVERSITY, HE WENT ON TO PUBLISH WORKS INCLUDING *HYPERBALLAD*, A BOOK OF ICELANDIC LANDSCAPE PHOTOGRAPHY. HOMMA'S WORK HAS BEEN PUBLISHED IN THE MAGAZINES *I-D*, LONDON, AND *RAY GUN*, SANTA MONICA. SOLO EXHIBITIONS INCLUDE "HYPERBALLAD IN REYKJAVIK, "SLEEP" AT THE TAKA ISHII GALLERY, TOKYO, AND "BABY LAND" AT THE PARCO GALLERY, TOKYO.

86-87 KAZUYA **SAKAKI**

ILLUSTRATION ENTITLED **SNOB AGAINST HOLY.** OBSESSIONS I HAVE NO OBSESSIONS, I WORK WITH LOYALTY AS MY INSPIRATION. MEANS NOTHING IN PARTICULAR. MATERIALS/DE-MATERIALS THIN PAPER, GOUACHE, LIQUITEX, BALL-POINT, MAGIC MARKER, AND SO ON. AUDIENCE NO LIMIT, EXCEPT ME – NO, PERHAPS ME TOO.
KAZUYA SAKAKI WAS BORN IN 1974 IN TOKUSHIMA, JAPAN. HE LIVES IN TOKYO, WORKING AS AN ILLUSTRATOR. HE HAS SHOWN HIS WORK IN EXHIBITIONS, INCLUDING A ONE-MAN SHOW IN KYOTO IN 1995, AND HAS WON AWARDS INCLUDING A BRONZE AND GOLD AT THE ANNUAL AWARDS OF THE CHOICE IN JAPAN.

88-89
NORIO NAKAMURA

NEWSPAPER ADVERTISING FOR A **FISH SKELETON-TYPE EXTENSION POWER CORD** FROM SONY. OBSTACLES SOCCER. MEANS MY BRAIN; MEANS WILL CHANGE FROM TIME TO TIME. MATERIALS/DE-MATERIALS MATERIALS I USE ARE GOOD IDEAS AND DE-MATERIALS ARE BAD IDEAS. AUDIENCE PEOPLE.

NORIO NAKAMURA WAS BORN IN KAWASAKI CITY, JAPAN IN 1967. AFTER GRADUATING FROM THE NIHON UNIVERSITY COLLEGE OF ART, HE JOINED FORMER CBS/SONY INC. [NOW KNOWN AS SONY MUSIC ENTERTAINMENT INC] WHERE HE WORKED AS AN ART DIRECTOR AND GRAPHIC DESIGNER. IN 1997 NAKAMURA ESTABLISHED HIS OWN OFFICE. HE HAS WON SEVERAL AWARDS INCLUDING A SILVER IN THE 76TH ANNUAL ART DIRECTORS CLUB AWARDS, AND THE SONY PLAYSTATION AWARDS '97 GOLDEN DISK AWARD.

90-91
GENTO MATSUMOTO

POP-UP COMPUTER. AN INTERACTIVE CD-ROM IN THE FORM OF A POP-UP BOOK ANIMATING LETTERS OF THE ALPHABET. OBSTACLES I HAVEN'T REALLY FOUND IT – LET'S SAY I DON'T HAVE ANY. MEANS THE DESIGN ENVIRONMENT HAS BEEN GETTING COMPLICATED LATELY. STAFF, LAYOUTS, MACHINES, NETWORKS – IT HAS BECOME DELICATE, BUT RIGHT NOW I'M KIND OF SATISFIED HERE. MATERIALS/DE-MATERIALS I DON'T REALLY STICK TO WHAT I USE – I JUST CHOOSE THE MATERIAL THAT FITS WHAT I WANT TO DO. AUDIENCE MAYBE, HOPEFULLY . . . GIRLS . . .

BORN IN 1961 IN TOKYO, GENTO MATSUMOTO GRADUATED FROM THE KUWASAWA INSTITUTE OF DESIGN IN 1983. HE FOUNDED SARU BRUNEI CO. LTD IN 1990 AFTER WORKING AT PROPELLOR ART WORKS. MATSUMOTO IS INVOLVED IN ART DIRECTION FOR MAGAZINES AND BOOKS, AND POSTER, LOGO AND FONT DESIGN. HE HAS WON SEVERAL AWARDS INCLUDING A MULTIMEDIA GRAND PRIX IN 1994.

93-95
KEISUKE OKI

BRAIN WAVE RIDER. A GAME MACHINE CONTROLLED BY COMMANDS ISSUED BY CHANGING BRAIN ACTIVITY. THE GAME USES IBVA [INTERACTIVE BRAINWAVE VISUAL ANALYZER] TO DETECT AND ANALYSE BRAIN WAVES VIA A MACINTOSH COMPUTER. DIRECTED AND PRODUCED BY DTI [KEISUKE OKI, YOSHIBUMI KAWAHARA]. PHOTOGRAPH COURTESY OF CANON ARTLAB. OBSTACLES MAN THE "MIND-HAVER" AND MINDLESS MACHINES. "WHEN I ADDRESS YOU, I INCLUDE US BOTH IN THE CLASS OF MIND-HAVERS" [DANIEL C. DENNETT, "KINDS OF MINDS"]. MEANS NATURAL AND ARTIFICIAL INTELLIGENCES. MATERIALS/DE-MATERIALS COMPLEXITIES IN OUR DAILY LIFE. AUDIENCE ALL THE MIND-HAVERS. KEISUKE OKI WAS BORN IN TOKYO IN 1952. AFTER GRADUATING FROM THE TAMA ART UNIVERSITY, HE WORKED AS AN ARTIST AND ALSO TAUGHT AT THE NAGOYA UNIVERSITY OF ART AND DESIGN. HIS WORK AT DTI [DIGITAL THERAPY INSTITUTE] INVOLVES CREATING PROJECTS THAT UTILIZE BRAINWAVES. OKI HAS EXHIBITED HIS WORK INTERNATIONALLY. IN 1998 HE MOVED TO PITTSBURGH, PENNSYLVANIA, TO BE A RESEARCH FELLOW AT THE STUDIO FOR CREATIVE INQUIRY AT CARNEGIE MELLON UNIVERSITY.

96
KATSUMI OMORI

PHOTOGRAPH FROM THE BOOK AND EXHIBITION **VERY SPECIAL LOVE** OF A WALL IN FRONT OF PACO STATION, MANILA CITY, THE PHILIPPINES, JANUARY 1997. OBSTACLES CHANGES OF THIS WORLD, CHANGES OF THE MOMENTS. MATERIALS/DE-MATERIALS CAMERAS, LENSES, LIGHTS, PHOTOGRAPHIC PRINTS. AUDIENCE SPICE GIRLS, PRODIGY AND VIOLENT GEISHA.

BORN IN KOBE, JAPAN IN 1963, KATSUMI OMORI STUDIED AT NIHON UNIVERSITY IN THE DEPARTMENT OF PHOTOGRAPHY. HE LEFT BEFORE COMPLETING THE COURSE TO TRAVEL THROUGH LATIN AMERICA TAKING PHOTOGRAPHS FOR A PORTFOLIO ENTITLED "GOOD TRIPS, BAD TRIPS" WHICH WON HIM THE ROBERT FRANK PRIZE. IN 1997 OMORI HAD A SOLO EXHIBITION "VERY SPECIAL LOVE", WHICH WAS LATER MADE INTO A BOOK. HE IS PRODUCING A PHOTO-STORY OF ROCK BAND SALSA GUM TAPE ORGANIZED BY PEOPLE IN THE HADANO AREA OF KANAGAWA PREFECTURE, JAPAN.

97
MAKOTO ORISAKI

HOLE WORKS. A PROJECT WHICH ALLOWS THE VIEWER TO SEE WHAT IS NOT VISIBLE, BUT IMPLIED. THE PROJECT WILL BE COMPLETED WHEN THE CONCEPT IS APPLIED TO A TANK AND A ROLLS ROYCE. THE PLASTIC DETERGENT BOTTLE WAS CHOSEN BECAUSE IT IS RECOGNIZABLE, AND A SYMBOL OF MODERN CIVILIZATION. OBSTACLES THE PROCESS OF THE SHIFT FROM PTOLEMAIC THEORY TO THE COPERNICAN THEORY AND THEN TO THE THEORY OF RELATIVITY. IT IS BECAUSE I HAVE NOTICED THAT ONLY THE SHIFT OF CONCEPTS LEADS US TO SOLUTIONS FOR ALL THE DIFFERENT PROBLEMS IN OUR DAILY LIFE. MEANS I AM LIVING A SERENE AND FRUGAL LIFE IN AN ATELIER. I RENOVATE THE INTERIOR, BUILD FURNITURE AND MAKE CLIPPINGS OF NEWSPAPER ARTICLES. I TRY TO CONSUME THE MINIMUM AND WORK THE MINIMUM. IN ORDER TO DISCOVER THE ESSENCE OF THINGS, MENTAL TRAINING IS NECESSARY. I USE A MACINTOSH COMPUTER EVERY DAY, AND CAMERAS. MATERIALS/DE-MATERIALS I CHOOSE MATERIALS RECOGNIZABLE FOR EVERYONE AND JUST PUT HOLES IN THEM TO SUGGEST A NEW WAY OF VIEWING THEM. AUDIENCE EVERYONE. MY WORK IS A MESSAGE TO THOSE WHO HAVE INNOVATIVE IDEAS AND VIEWS OF THE WORLD; TO STIMULATE AND AWAKEN THE BIG-HEADED ECONOMIC ANIMALS.

BORN IN 1965 IN SAITAMA, JAPAN, MAKOTO ORISAKI STUDIED ELECTRONICS FOR FIVE YEARS AT UNIVERSITY BEFORE DECIDING TO BECOME A DESIGNER. IN 1989 HE GRADUATED FROM THE KWAZAWA INSTITUTE OF DESIGN AND BEGAN WORKING WITH YUKIMASA OKUMURA AT THE STUDIO IN TOKYO. IN 1991 HE STARTED WORK AS A FREELANCE DESIGNER AND NOW WORKS IN A NUMBER OF DISCIPLINES INCLUDING FINE ART, GRAPHIC DESIGN, PACKAGING, PRODUCT AND INTERIOR DESIGN. LIVING WHAT HE DESCRIBES AS A "SERENE AND FRUGAL LIFE", HIS AIM IS TO TREAT DESIGN LESS AS A VEHICLE FOR PERSONAL EXPRESSION, AND MORE AS AN ACTIVITY INVOLVING RESPONSIBILITY TO SOCIETY.

98-99
ICHIRO TANIDA

JOHN AND JANE DOE, INC. COMPUTER GRAPHICS PART OF A SERIES OF COMPUTER-GENERATED IMAGES CREATED FOR JAPANESE CLIENTS. OBSTACLES COMPLICATED PROCESS [MANUFACTURING], SIMPLE RESULT. MEANS I HAVEN'T THOUGHT ABOUT IT, SO I DON'T KNOW. MATERIALS/DE-MATERIALS HANDS. AUDIENCE MYSELF.

ICHIRO TANIDA WAS BORN IN 1965 IN TOKYO. AFTER GRADUATING FROM THE TOKYO SCHOOL OF ART IN 1986, HE WORKED WITH HIROKI TANIGUCHI AS AN ASSISTANT BEFORE GOING FREELANCE IN 1992. IN 1994 HE ESTABLISHED JOHN AND JANE DOE, INC. WORKING PREDOMINANTLY IN COMPUTER GRAPHICS, DESIGNING CD COVERS, TELEVISION GRAPHICS AND MUSIC VIDEOS. HE HAS BEEN RECOGNIZED FOR HIS WORK INTERNATIONALLY AND HAS RECEIVED SEVERAL AWARDS.

100-101
NORIYUKI TANAKA

100 **SCREAM OF THE NEW GENERATION.** POSTER. 101 ART BOOK CALLED **KISEKAE NINGEN DAIICHIGO**, A COLLABORATION BETWEEN ARTIST YASUMASA MORIMURA AND NORIYUKI TANAKA. OBSTACLES ADVANCING THE BOUNDARIES OF HIS OWN REALM OF PRESENTATION AS A GROUND-BREAKING INNOVATOR, CREATING EXPRESSIONS WHICH EVOLVE FROM HIS BODY INTO VARIOUS MEDIA AND TRYING TO BOND ART AND SOCIETY THROUGH HIS WORK. MEANS TANAKA EXPLORES THE ESSENCE OF ART THROUGH COLLABORATIONS WITH OTHER DISCIPLINES, SUCH AS SCIENCE, USING THESE AS TOOLS. HE HAS EXPANDED HIS ACTIVITIES INTO INSTALLATION, PAINTING, GRAPHIC DESIGN, PHOTOGRAPHY, INTERIOR DESIGN, COMPUTER GRAPHICS, SCULPTURE AND ARCHITECTURE. NORIYUKI TANAKA WORKS WITH A COMBINATION OF PERFORMANCE, PAINTING, INSTALLATION, ARCHITECTURE AND MULTIMEDIA UNDER THE UMBRELLA NORIYUKI TANAKA ACTIVITY. HE WAS THE ART DIRECTOR FOR ASIAN LOCATION WORK ON PETER GREENAWAY'S FILM *THE PILLOW BOOK*. HE IS RESPONSIBLE FOR RENAISSANCE GENERATION, A SUPPORT SYSTEM FOR CREATORS WHO CHALLENGE THE CONVENTIONAL BORDERS OF SCIENCE, TECHNOLOGY, ART AND DESIGN. HE HAS WON MANY AWARDS AND HAS EXHIBITED AND PUBLISHED SEVERAL WORKS INCLUDING *THE ART OF CLEAR LIGHT* AND *INSPIRATION OF NORIYUKI TANAKA*.

102-103
TAMANO TETSUYA

INDEPENDENT PROJECT CONCERNED WITH EXPRESSING HUMAN EXPERIENCE AND EMOTION IN A VISUAL AND AUDIO MANNER. OBSTACLES FINDING A PURE FORM OF EXPRESSING WHAT HAPPENS IN THE MIND. MEANS INTERACTING WITH ARTISTS FROM ALL OVER THE WORLD: FABRICA [THE ITALIAN ART INSTITUTE] IS A PLACE WHERE AN "INTERCOURSE OF EXPRESSION" IS POSSIBLE. MATERIALS/DE-MATERIALS MY MODELS ARE MAINLY FRIENDS. I USE A POWER MACINTOSH ETC. WHAT IS INVISIBLE – OR CAUSES TROUBLE WHEN SEEN – IS WHAT CONSTRUCTS THE MAIN PART OF THIS WORK. AUDIENCE THE PEOPLE WHO HAVE THE CHANCE TO SEE MY WORK; THAT IS A VERY NATURAL PHENOMENON. WHAT I AM TRYING TO DO IS JUST SUGGEST.

TAMANO TETSUYA WAS BORN IN SAITAMA, JAPAN. IN 1997 HE RECEIVED A SCHOLARSHIP TO STUDY AT THE ITALIAN ART INSTITUTE FABRICA. HE HAS WON SEVERAL PRIZES FOR HIS ARTISTIC ENDEAVOURS, INCLUDING THE GRAND PRIX IN JACA '96 [JAPAN VISUAL ART EXIBITIA]. HIS WORK HAS BEEN EXHIBITED IN RUSSIA, BRAZIL, MALAYSIA, VIETNAM, HONG KONG AND CHINA.

104-105
YASUKO YOSHIDA

DIGITAL ILLUSTRATIONS OF JAPANESE GIRLS OR **MY-COS** BASED ON TRADITIONAL JAPANESE FEMALE DANCERS. YOSHIDA PLANS TO CREATE "A FUNNY IMPRESSIVE STORY WITH THOSE CHARACTERS" AND WOULD LIKE TO MENTION THAT SHE IS ALSO "A CUTE KYO-BIJIN" [A BEAUTY FROM KYOTO] HERSELF. OBSTACLES I ALWAYS MAKE MUCH OF A FLASH IDEA, A POINT OF VIEW, TOUCH, STORY, LOVELINESS AND BEAUTY. MEANS WHEN I LEFT A COMMERCIALS PRODUCTION COMPANY THREE YEARS AGO, I GOT UNEMPLOYMENT INSURANCE. I DECIDED TO BUY SOMETHING FOR MY BENEFIT – AN INVESTMENT IN MYSELF. THAT WAS AN APPLE MACINTOSH. MATERIALS/DE-MATERIALS MY MAIN TOOL FOR CREATING IS THE COMPUTER. SOMETIMES I DRAW ILLUSTRATION BY HAND. USING A COMPUTER I CAN CREATE A MOVIE BY MYSELF! THAT'S A BIG ADVANTAGE. AUDIENCE PEOPLE ALL OVER THE WORLD.

AFTER ATTENDING THE KYOTO SEIKA UNIVERSITY SCHOOL OF DESIGN AND VISUAL COMMUNICATION, YASUKO YOSHIDA WORKED FOR A COMMERCIAL PRODUCTION COMPANY. THREE YEARS AGO SHE BEGAN FREELANCING AS A "VISUAL CREATOR". SHE HAS SINCE WON THE TOWA TEI MADIA REMIX CONTEST GRAND-PRIX AND THE HYPERLIB CG CONTEST. YOSHIDA ALSO WORKS FOR A GAMES AND COMPUTER GRAPHICS COMPANY CALLED MULTIES. HER MAIN WORK IS IN CD-ROM PRODUCTION, TELEVISION GRAPHICS, INTERNET DESIGN AND MUSIC GRAPHICS.

MEXICO

108 FAKIR

FAKIR MAGAZINE, A HAND-CRAFTED ART OBJECT MADE WITH DIVERSE MEDIA, WITH A LIMITED PRINT RUN OF 100 PER ISSUE. ᴏᴏᴛᴇᴄᴄɪᴏɴᴇ AT TIMES THE NEED TO BE CREATIVE BECOMES AN ITCH; WHEN ONE DECIDES TO SATISFY THE ITCH SOMETHING AKIN TO *FAKIR* CAN BE BORN, WITH NOTHING MORE IN MIND THAN TO DESIGN FREELY. ᴍᴇᴏɴᴇ IN MEXICO CLIENTS DON'T TAKE RISKS, AND SEEM TO LIMIT DESIGNERS TO FOLLOWING CERTAIN INTERNATIONAL TRENDS. OUR BEST OPTION TO EXPERIMENT WAS TO MAKE A PUBLICATION. IT'S A GOOD EXCUSE TO GET TOGETHER AND CHANGE THE WORLD, TO HAVE SOME BEERS AND DANCE WHILE A BRAINSTORMING IS HAPPENING. ᴍᴏᴛᴇᴏɪᴏɪᴄ/ᴏᴇᴍᴏᴛᴇᴏɪᴏɪᴄ WE START BY DOING SOME SKETCHES AND DISCUSSING IDEAS, THEN WE MOVE ON TO COMPUTER. MOST OF THE MAGAZINE IS PRINTED ON A BLACK AND WHITE LASER PRINTER ON USED PAPER. A LOT OF *FAKIR* IS MADE FROM GARBAGE, SUCH AS POSITIVES FROM PRE PRESS WASTE, BACK ISSUES OF *READER'S DIGEST*, NAPKINS FROM A CANTINA, BEER LABELS . . .

FAKIR IS A HAND-CRAFTED MAGAZINE, FASHIONED IN A TRADITION THAT UTILIZES THE RESOURCES AT HAND, REUSABLE MATERIALS THAT ACCENTUATE THE VERNACULAR SPIRIT COMMONLY BROUGHT TO LIFE IN CHEAP, GARBAGE LITERATURE. "WE WENT DIRECTLY TO THE STREETS AND INVESTIGATED THE COMMON THINGS IN LIFE, USING ONLY HORSEPLAY AND FUN AS OUR METHOD OF SELECTION, TO FIND CLUES THAT IN ANOTHER CONTEXT ACQUIRE A NEW SYMBOLISM". *FAKIR* IS CREATED BY JAVIER CABALLERO, DIANA PATRICIA GONZALEZ, JUANJO BUSTOS AND RAFAEL BENITEZ. IT IS AN UNDERGROUND ZINE IN MEXICO AND WAS SUPPLIED BY *MATIZ* MAGAZINE, A PUBLICATION THAT PROMOTES MEXICAN GRAPHIC DESIGNERS.

109 IGNACIO PEON

DRAWING FROM A SELF-PUBLISHED MAGAZINE ENTITLED **FEA** [MEANING UGLY] WHICH EXPLORES THEMES OF MEXICAN VERNACULAR. ᴏᴏᴛᴇᴄᴄɪᴏɴᴇ IMPERFECTIONS IN GENERAL: A TYPE BADLY DRAWN, A DOODLE AT THE EDGE OF MY NOTEBOOK, A STREET POSTER, ANY STUFF THAT LOOKS HAND MADE AND NOT MACHINE CREATED. ᴍᴇᴏɴᴇ MORE THAN TEN TELEVISION CHANNELS TO WATCH AND A REMOTE CONTROL. MY MAC WITH THREE DIFFERENT PROGRAMS OPEN, MY SKETCHBOOK, THE LATEST ISSUE OF MY FAVOURITE MAGAZINE, ALL TURNED ON OR OPEN AT THE SAME TIME. MEDIA SATURATION MAKES MY HEAD SPIN AND ENABLES MY IDEAS TO FLOW AT THE SAME SPEED I CLICK THE MOUSE. ᴍᴏᴛᴇᴏɪᴏɪᴄ/ᴏᴇᴍᴏᴛᴇᴏɪᴏɪᴄ AN OLD SKETCHBOOK, A BRUSH, A FOUNTAIN PEN AND SOME INK. ᴏᴜᴍᴇᴏᴄᴇ OTHER DESIGNERS.

IGNACIO PEON LIVES AND WORKS IN MEXICO CITY. HE STUDIED FOR HIS BACHELOR OF FINE ARTS DEGREE AT THE UNIVERSIDAD IBEROAMERICANA. HE IS CO-FOUNDER OF INDEPENDENT PUBLISHING HOUSE EDITORIAL PELLEJO, WHERE HE CO-CREATED THE EXPERIMENTAL MAGAZINES *NUMERO X* AND *FEA*. SINCE 1995 HE HAS WORKED FOR THE TELEVISION COMPANY TELEVISA, DESIGNING LOGOS FOR DIFFERENT PROGRAMMES. IN 1995 HE DESIGNED THE CHANNEL 9 IDENTITY. HE ALSO DESIGNS THEIR SPORTS GRAPHICS. HE HAS PARTICIPATED IN DESIGN EXHIBITIONS AND WRITES FOR THE DESIGN MAGAZINE *MATIZ*. HE HAS WORKED ON OTHER MAGAZINES INCLUDING *GOLEM*, *THE O*, *COMPLOT INTERNACIONAL* AND *LABERINTO URBANO*.

110-111 MÓNICA PEÓN DÍAZ **BARRIGA**

110 **BEMBOLIO**. FROM A 3D ANIMATION IN WHICH ORGANIC AND SYNTHETIC FORMS COMBINE INTO ONE IMPROBABLE DANCING LIFEFORM. 111 **BE HERE, BE NEAR**. FROM A PERFORMANCE PRESENTED INSIDE A HIDDEN DUNGEON ON A RAINY NIGHT. ᴏᴏᴛᴇᴄᴄɪᴏɴᴇ THE CLASHING OR MEETING POINT BETWEEN THE ORGANIC AND THE SYNTHETIC, ARTIFICIAL LIFE. THE CREATION OF IMMERSIVE EXPERIENCES. ᴍᴇᴏɴᴇ HAVING TO RE-INVENT MYSELF WHILE AT CRANBROOK BUT WITHOUT FORGETTING WHERE I CAME FROM. BEING EXPOSED TO MORE ADVANCED TECHNOLOGY AND LITERARY THEORY. ᴍᴏᴛᴇᴏɪᴏɪᴄ/ᴏᴇᴍᴏᴛᴇᴏɪᴏɪᴄ INTEGRATING HAND-MADE OBJECTS WITH 3D COMPUTER ANIMATION.

MÓNICA PEÓN DÍAZ BARRIGA WAS BORN IN 1969 IN MEXICO CITY. SHE ATTENDED THE UNIVERSIDAD AUTÓNOMA METROPOLITANA, MEXICO CITY, GRADUATING WITH A DEGREE IN GRAPHIC DESIGN IN 1992. SHE HAS ALSO WORKED FOR THE GLOBAL ENTERPRISE SERVICES INTERNET, MEXICO CITY, WHERE SHE DESIGNED AND ART DIRECTED WEB PAGES. PRIOR TO THIS SHE ART DIRECTED MAGAZINES SUCH AS *THE O*, *COMPLOT INTERNACIONAL* AND *BABEL*. SHE RECEIVED HER MASTER OF FINE ARTS DEGREE IN DESIGN AT THE CRANBROOK ACADEMY OF ART IN 1998, AND PLANS AN INTERNSHIP WITH STUDIO DUMBAR IN THE NETHERLANDS.

THE NETHERLANDS

114-115 KESSELS**KRAMER**

PLACEMATS AND COMPLIMENTARY TRAVEL KIT FOR VISITORS TO THE **HANS BRINKER BUDGET HOTEL**. THE CUT-OUT TOILETRIES KIT SUPPLIES ARTICLES SUCH AS SOAP AND A HAIRDRYER. ᴏᴏᴛᴇᴄᴄɪᴏɴᴇ OUR OBSESSIONS BEGIN SOMEWHERE OUT BEYOND, IN BACKYARDS OF GRASSY GREEN, WHERE LITTLE DOGGIES PLAY. WE LIKE THE SWINGS. YOU WILL SEE US THERE. ᴍᴇᴏɴᴇ LITTLE INFLATABLE POOLS. ᴍᴏᴛᴇᴏɪᴏɪᴄ A GOOD SENSIBLE PAIR OF SHOES. ᴏᴇᴍᴏᴛᴇᴏɪᴏɪᴄ WE'VE REJECTED ALL USE OF THE SLINKY, FOR NOW. ᴏᴜᴍᴇᴏᴄᴇ GARDEN GNOMES FROM UTAH. AND THAT BASEBALL TEAM IN ALASKA, THE MOOSES.

LESS OF AN ADVERTISING AGENCY AND MORE OF A "CREATIVE THINK TANK", KESSELSKRAMER IS THE BABY OF FORMER DOG TRAINER JOHAN KRAMER AND DENTAL STUDENT/FOOTBALL FANATIC ERIK KESSELS. THE COMPANY IS BASED IN AMSTERDAM AND OPENED IN JANUARY 1996. KESSELSKRAMER HAS A STAFF OF TWELVE AND WORKS IN FIELDS INCLUDING ADVERTISING, EDITORIAL AND GRAPHIC DESIGN. THE COMPANY'S CLIENT LIST INCLUDES LEVI'S, NIKE AND CHANNEL 5. THEIR WORK FOR THE HANS BRINKER BUDGET HOTEL, AMSTERDAM, CAPITAL FM AND NIKE EUROPE HAS APPEARED IN D&AD ANNUALS. THEY WON EPICA AWARDS FOR HANS BRINKER AND NIKE EUROPE, AND BEST OF SHOW IN 1997 AT THE NEW YORK ART DIRECTORS CLUB FOR THEIR CAPITAL FM CAMPAIGN "STATIC".

118-119 André **THIJSSEN**

TWO PHOTOGRAPHS. 118 **RIGHT EYE**, TAKEN FOR THE ARTIST AT THE ACADEMIC HOSPITAL IN AMSTERDAM, DEPARTMENT OF EYE RESEARCH. 119 PICTURE OF A PHOTOGRAPH FOUND IN A SOUTH ARIZONA SHRINE AMONGST CANDLES IN A CHAPEL, INTIMATING THAT THE **BABY** IS PROBABLY DEAD. ᴏᴏᴛᴇᴄᴄɪᴏɴᴇ THE ODD, THE UNUSUAL, APPROACHING THE CLICHÉ FROM AN UNEXPECTED ANGLE, BEING HIGHLY FLEXIBLE IN LINKING ONE THOUGHT WITH THE LEAST OBVIOUS. ᴍᴇᴏɴᴇ AN UNSTOPPABLE DRIVE! MOST OF THIS MATERIAL IS OBTAINED WHILE TRAVELLING, I REALLY USE MY EYES, PUT SCENES IN ANOTHER CONTEXT — THAT IS HOW I THINK WHILE I'M LOOKING AROUND. ᴍᴏᴛᴇᴏɪᴏɪᴄ/ᴏᴇᴍᴏᴛᴇᴏɪᴏɪᴄ ANY KIND OF MATERIAL IS WELCOME IN PRINCIPLE. PHOTOGRAPHY, MANIPULATED VIA THE MACINTOSH OR NOT, IS MAINLY USED BUT IF IT IS DESIRED TO EXPRESS A THOUGHT VIA A SELF-MADE [AND AFTERWARDS PHOTOGRAPHED] 3-D SCULPTURE, EVEN A TURD MIGHT BE WELCOME. ᴏᴜᴍᴇᴏᴄᴇ THE LIKE-MINDED.

ANDRÉ THIJSSEN WAS BORN IN 1948 IN VLAARDINGEN, THE NETHERLANDS. HE IS A SELF-TAUGHT GRAPHIC DESIGNER/IMAGE MAKER, EXHIBITING HIS WORK IN GALLERIES WORLDWIDE. HE HAS ALSO BEEN A GUEST LECTURER AT VARIOUS INSTITUTIONS INCLUDING THE SCHOOL FOR THE VISUAL ARTS IN NEW YORK, THE ROYAL ACADEMY FOR THE FINE ARTS IN THE HAGUE, AND THE ROYAL ACADEMY FOR THE FINE ARTS IN GHENT, BELGIUM. THIJSSEN HAS RECEIVED AWARDS IN THE NETHERLANDS, THE UK AND THE USA.

NORWAY

122 HALVOR **BODIN**

MUSIC CD **HIMMELTITTER** FOR NORWEGIAN ROCK BAND CC COWBOYS. ᴏᴏᴛᴇᴄᴄɪᴏɴᴇ I BELIEVE IN THE IRRATIONAL INTUITION, AND ALL THE SMALL AND BIG THINGS WE DO NOT SEE OR UNDERSTAND. I SEARCH FOR THE BEAUTY IN PERFECTIONISM AND TRY TO PUSH THE LIMITS TOWARDS THE UNEXPECTED. DESIGN OR DIE. ᴍᴇᴏɴᴇ I NEED FAST INTERNET ACCESS, MY G3, POST-IT PADS, BLACK MARKERS, A XEROX COPIER, VIDEO CAMERA, STILL CAMERA, NIGHT SHIFTS, VEGETARIAN FOOD OR SUSHI. I HATE FREQUENT AND LONG MEETINGS WITH CLIENTS, I HATE THE TELEPHONE.

HALVOR BODIN WAS BORN IN 1964 IN LILLEHAMMER, NORWAY. HE WAS A FILM PRODUCER BEFORE FOUNDING FAVOLA FILM WITH THOMAS ROBSAHM TOGNAZZI IN 1989. WITH NO FORMAL TRAINING, HE PRACTISED GRAPHIC DESIGN WITH VARIOUS GROUPS, AND IN 1995 FORMED UNION DESIGN. UNION DESIGN WORK IN PRINT, WEB DESIGN, CD-ROM, PACKAGING AND TELEVISION ANIMATION, WITH CLIENTS INCLUDING THE COCA-COLA COMPANY, PETROLEUM GEO SERVICES AND CHASE MANHATTAN.

123 MARIUS **WATZ**

FRAME FROM **WORM**, A PIECE OF ANIMATION FEATURING CUSTOM SOFTWARE. ᴏᴏᴛᴇᴄᴄɪᴏɴᴇ MAKE THE IMAGE NEVER STOP MOVING. WHY DRAW ONE FLOWER WHEN YOU CAN DRAW A MILLION? ᴍᴇᴏɴᴇ ACCESS TO COMPUTERS AND COMPUTER-CONTROLLABLE DEVICES. PEOPLE WHO LOVE WHAT THEY'RE DOING. TELECOMMUNICATIONS EQUIPMENT — IT'S GOOD TO TALK. ᴍᴏᴛᴇᴏɪᴏɪᴄ/ᴏᴇᴍᴏᴛᴇᴏɪᴏɪᴄ AVOID ANYTHING THAT RESTRICTS YOU, BE IT SOFTWARE, HARDWARE, PEOPLE OR PLACES. USE TOOLS THAT CAN BE DE-PROGRAMMED AND RE-APPROPRIATED FOR NEW PURPOSES. DUMB OBJECTS CAN BE MADE SMART. ᴏᴜᴍᴇᴏᴄᴇ ANYONE WHO LOVES.

MARIUS WATZ IS A GRAPHIC DESIGNER AND PROGRAMMER WORKING IN NEW AND OLD MEDIA. HE USES CUSTOM-DEVELOPED SOFTWARE TO CREATE DESIGNS FOR 2D, 3D AND 4D AS WELL AS REALTIME SOUND WITH GRAPHICS. HIS FOCUS IS ANIMATION AND MULTIMEDIA, BRANCHING INTO PRINT AND INSTALLATION WORK. HE WORKS UNDER THE NAME AMOEBA [THE EVOLUTIONARY] TRYING TO MIX COMMERCIAL WORK WITH ARTISTIC AND EDUCATIONAL PROJECTS.

126-127 PIOTR SZYHALSKI

ACIDITY. FROM THE ARTIST'S WEBSITE. MEANS TEACHING [TO BE ABLE TO SURVIVE WHILE ENTERTAINING MY TRUE INTEREST: MAKING THINGS] I TEACH BECAUSE I FIND IT INCREDIBLY FULFILLING AND STIMULATING, AND IT PROVIDES A CHALLENGING CONTEXT IN WHICH I AM FORCED TO OBSERVE MY OWN WORK. I DO ALL MY PERSONAL WORK AT HOME: THE CONCEPT OF COMMUNICATING WITH THE "GLOBAL AUDIENCE" FROM THE TINY LOFT AT OUR APARTMENT IS EXCITING AND HIGHLIGHTS THE IDEA OF INTIMACY POSSIBLE THROUGH THE WEB. MATERIALS/NONMATERIALS THE "MAKE DO" TRADITION IN ART I LEARNED GROWING UP IN POLAND WHERE THE LUXURY OF FANCY ART SUPPLIES WAS VIRTUALLY NON-EXISTENT. THE KEY DISCOVERY: RESPECT FOR THE MATERIALS ONE DID HAVE AT HAND, AND THEN THE SAME ATTENTION GIVEN TO THE LEFTOVER MATERIALS. MATERIALS I REJECT? I CAN HONESTLY SAY THAT THERE AREN'T ANY – I AM POLISH, REALLY NOTHING SHOULD GO TO WASTE. AUDIENCE THE PERCEPTION OF GOOD ARTWORK CAN BE CHARACTERIZED BY COMMON EXPERIENCES. WORK IS SUBJECTIVE BUT IN MANY WAYS IT DRAWS FROM THE ONGOING STRUGGLE FOR OBJECTIVITY. THIS IS WHERE THE AUDIENCE RESOLVES THE CONFLICT – THROUGH THE MULTIPLE INTERPRETATIONS DEFINING THE OBJECTIVE MEANINGS OF THE WORK.
PIOTR SZYHALSKI MOVED TO THE USA FROM POLAND IN 1990. HE HOLDS MASTER OF FINE ARTS DEGREES IN DRAWING AND POSTER DESIGN FROM THE ACADEMY OF VISUAL ARTS IN POZNAN, POLAND. HE TEACHES AT THE MINNEAPOLIS COLLEGE OF ART AND DESIGN. ONE OF HIS COURSES EXPOSES STUDENTS TO HISTORICAL AND CONTEMPORARY CONCEPTS OF PROPAGANDA. MOVING BETWEEN FINE ART AND DESIGN, HE HAS EXHIBITED HIS WORK INTERNATIONALLY AND PRODUCED ART ON THE INTERNET, MOST NOTABLY "THE SPLEEN" WHICH HAS RECEIVED MANY AWARDS.

130-131 ORANGE JUICE DESIGN

TWO PAGES FROM I-JUSI MAGAZINE. 130 TRADITIONAL HEALERS, COMMENTS ON AFRICAN "ALTERNATIVE MEDICINE" AND THE CONFLICT BETWEEN WESTERN AND TRADITIONAL AFRICAN MEDICINE. 131 BOYS TO MEN A COLLAGE OF STREET SIGNS AND RELATED IMAGES COMMENTING ON VIOLENCE IN SOUTH AFRICA [USUALLY BLACK ON BLACK] WHERE MOST PERPETRATORS ARE YOUNG BOYS AND MEN. OBSESSIONS STAYING SMALL AND HANDS-ON. DESIGNING IN A STYLE THAT REFLECTS MY ROOTS, USING LOCAL VERNACULAR AS INSPIRATION. PROMOTING YOUNG TALENT, TRAVEL, ARCHITECTURE, GOOD FOOD [AND WINE] AND RIDING MY BICYCLE. MEANS MEGA-POWERFUL MAC SYSTEM WITH ALL THE BELLS AND WHISTLES; REASONABLY SAFE ACCESS TO "DESIGN ON THE STREETS" OF DURBAN [BY CONTRAST JOHANNESBURG STREETS ARE UNSAFE FOR A LONE WHITE MAN AND CAPE TOWN HAS LITTLE STREET DESIGN]; A FREE AND DEMOCRATIC [SORT OF] SOUTH AFRICA; AN AMAZING "STREET VIBE"; AND GOOD SUNNY AFRICAN WEATHER. MATERIALS/NONMATERIALS MEGA-POWERFUL MAC SYSTEM, "SNAPMATIC" CAMERA AND ONE HOUR PHOTOLABS, A CAR [FOR A QUICK GETAWAY], "AS FOUND" GRAPHIC DESIGN, AND JUST GOOD PLAIN OBSERVATION. AUDIENCE ANYONE WHO LIKES MY KIND OF DESIGN VIEW; FELLOW "AFRICAN INSPIRED" DESIGNERS [I'M TRYING TO GET LOCAL SOUTH AFRICAN DESIGNERS TO REALIZE THE MAGIC IN THEIR OWN BACKYARD].
ORANGE JUICE DESIGN OPENED IN 1995 WITH ONE EMPLOYEE, GARTH WALKER, AND NO CLIENTS. TODAY ORANGE JUICE HAS THREE OFFICES [DURBAN, CAPE TOWN AND JOHANNESBURG] WITH A STAFF OF 21, AND OPERATES AS PART OF OGILVY & MATHER SOUTH AFRICA. ONE AIM IS TO DEVELOP A TRUE "AFRICAN" STYLE WITH CLIENTS INCLUDING AUDI, VOLKSWAGEN AND SHELL. I-JUSI IS A MAGAZINE DEVELOPED BY ORANGE JUICE DESIGN, WHICH SERVES TO PROMOTE A GRAPHIC LANGUAGE ROOTED IN THEIR OWN AFRICAN EXPERIENCE. AS A STARTING POINT I-JUSI USES ICONS, CRAFTWORK AND INDIGENOUS SIGNAGE FOUND ON THE STREETS AND PRODUCED BY ORDINARY [MOSTLY] BLACK/INDIAN STREET TRADERS.

134-135 PIERRE KELLER

TWO PHOTOGRAPHS. 134 BRAZILIAN ASS, SÃO PAULO. 135 CHELSEA HOTEL /BATH TUB, NEW YORK. OBSESSIONS SEX, BORDEAUX WINES, SEX. MEANS STRONG AND UNUSUAL SITUATIONS. MATERIALS MEN/WOMEN; WHY NOT? AUDIENCE EGOCENTRIC – I FIRST WANT TO BE SURPRISED BY MY OWN WORK, THEN FOR MY OWN PLEASURE I LIKE TO BE ABLE TO RECONSTRUCT SITUATIONS FROM THESE IMAGES, AND ENJOY THEM AGAIN. PIERRE KELLER WAS BORN IN 1945 IN MÖNCHALTORF, SWITZERLAND. SINCE 1968 HE HAS WORKED AS AN ARTIST IN A WIDE RANGE OF DISCIPLINES BOTH IN SWITZERLAND AND ABROAD. FOR 12 YEARS HE WORKED IN NEW YORK AS AN ART CONSULTANT ON THE FRINGES OF ANDY WARHOL'S FACTORY. MOST RECENTLY HE HAS SERVED AS DIRECTOR OF ECOLE CANTONALE D'ART DE LAUSANNE [ECAL]. HE HAS ALSO ESTABLISHED A GALLERY IN LAUSANNE.

138-141 OPTIMO

TWO FONT DESIGNS. 138-139 KABIN, BASED ON A MULTIPURPOSE HOUSING SYSTEM, AS IT APPEARED IN WELCOMEX MAGAZINE, DESIGNED BY STEPHANE DELGADO AND GILLES GAVILLET. 140-141 DETROIT. THIS MULTIPLE-MASTER FONT WAS CREATED DURING A VISIT TO CRANBROOK ACADEMY OF ART. INTENDED TO BE USED "BY EVERY SALESMAN IN DOWNTOWN DETROIT", IT IS USED THROUGHOUT THIS BOOK. OBSESSIONS TO CIRCULATE THE RUMOUR THAT TYPOGRAPHY IS ALIVE. MEANS THERE IS HERE A LACK OF CONTENT. MATERIALS/NONMATERIALS INSPIRATION, EXPIRATION. AUDIENCE ALEX ATTIAS, ANGELO BENEDETTO, EVA BOURQUIN, MILENA CHIMENTI, CHIC RECORDINGS, LA COUPOLE [BIENNE], ANNE CRAUSAZ, PATRICK DAVID, ROBERTO DEL NAJA, DIANE DE SAUGY, MICHAEL HISBERGER, FABRICE JACOT, PAUL KIRPS, SEB KOHLER, KURT THE HACKER, LE LOTUS, MICHAEL ET MATTHIAS, NOTORIOUS B.I.G., LAURIE MAKELA, SCOTT MAKELA, JOSEF M BROCKMAN, SHUGGIE OTIS, OUR FAMILIES, NICOLE UDRY, FRANCOIS RAPPO, RAPHAEL SEBBAG, JAN SEVENSTER, ABBA SHANTI, TRANSAM, ACHILLE, ALEXANDRE, STELIO TZONIS, CORNEL WINDLIN.
STEPHANE DELGADO, GILLES GAVILLET AND DAVID RUST ARE ALL FORMER STUDENTS FROM THE ECOLE CANTONALE D'ART DE LAUSANNE. THEY WORK TOGETHER AS OPTIMO IN THEIR STUDIO IN SWITZERLAND.

144-145 ANTHONY BURRILL

COVER AND SPREAD FROM SWEET SHOP, A LIMITED-EDITION, SELF-PUBLISHED ART BOOK, BASED ON THE SENSATION OF SEEING THE WORLD THROUGH FRESH EYES – THE WORLD IS A GIANT SWEET SHOP. OBSESSIONS PHOTOCOPIERS [FIVE PENCE IN CORNER SHOPS], OLD TECHNOLOGY, CEEFAX, CASIO ORGANS, EARLY ELECTRONIC MUSIC, ATM DISPLAY SCREENS, TITLE SEQUENCES FROM TELEVISION PROGRAMMES I GREW UP WITH. MEANS ACCESS TO MY COLLECTION OF CLIP-ART BOOKS, OLD CATALOGUES, TYPE SAMPLES AND PHOTOCOPIER SHOPS. MATERIALS/NONMATERIALS PHOTOCOPIES CUT OUT WITH SCISSORS AND STUCK TOGETHER WITH PRITT STICK. SOMETIMES I USE A COMPUTER. I DON'T CHOOSE TO 'NOT' USE ANY MATERIALS. AUDIENCE PEOPLE WHO CAN RELATE TO THE WORLD I GREW UP IN AND TO MY OWN PERSONAL OBSESSIONS. I LIKE TO MAKE PEOPLE LAUGH; HUMOUR IS A GOOD WAY TO COMMUNICATE. I SEE MY AUDIENCE AS QUITE SMALL, BUT LOYAL. ANTHONY BURRILL WAS BORN IN ENGLAND IN 1966. HE STUDIED AT LEEDS POLYTECHNIC AND THEN ACQUIRED A MASTER OF ARTS IN GRAPHIC DESIGN FROM THE ROYAL COLLEGE OF ART, LONDON. HE WORKS FOR CLIENTS INCLUDING MTV EUROPE AND ADVERTISING AGENCIES IN THE UK AND THE NETHERLANDS. EMBRACING PRINT, TELEVISION, AND INTERNET DESIGN. HIS PERSONAL PROJECTS INCLUDE THE PRODUCTION OF LIMITED-EDITION ART BOOKS. IN 1996 BURRILL WAS RECOGNIZED FOR HIS TESCO INTERNET WEBSITE BY CREATIVE REVIEW MAGAZINE AND INCLUDED IN THE EXHIBITION "CREATIVE FUTURES".

146-147 DAVID CROW

SCREEN GRABS FROM **FOREST OF SIGNS**, A MULTIMEDIA INTERPRETA-
TION OF SIGNAGE CREATED WITH MIKE WILLIAMS AND PUBLISHED BY
RESEARCH PUBLISHING, 1998. **OBSESSIONS** I SPEND A LOT OF TIME
THINKING ABOUT THE WAY THAT [VISUAL] LANGUAGE IS USED AS A
MEANS OF CONTROL. I LIKE TO READ SEMIOTIC THEORIES, IN PARTICULAR
ROLAND BARTHES. **MEANS** AS A LECTURER, MY TIME IS COMMITTED TO
TEACHING, EITHER DIRECTLY OR INDIRECTLY. MY PERSONAL WORK IS DONE
LARGELY AS RESEARCH ACTIVITY THROUGH THE ART SCHOOL HERE IN
LIVERPOOL **MATERIALS/NONMATERIALS** I USE PHOTOGRAPHY, TYPOG-
RAPHY AND SOFTWARE. **AUDIENCE** GIVEN THAT THE WORK IS
RESEARCH BASED RATHER THAN COMMERCIAL, THE AUDIENCE IS USUALLY
STUDENTS IN THE VISUAL ARTS, OR FELLOW PRACTITIONERS. OF COURSE,
THE WORK OFTEN INVOLVES PLACING VISUALS IN PUBLIC SPACES SO THE
AUDIENCE FOR THIS PART OF THE WORK IS MUCH BROADER.
DAVID CROW WAS BORN IN GALASHIELS, SCOTLAND IN 1962 AND GRADUATED IN
GRAPHIC DESIGN FROM MANCHESTER POLYTECHNIC IN 1985. HE WAS THE IN-
HOUSE DESIGNER FOR ISLAND RECORDS AND HAS WORKED FREELANCE FOR
ROLLING STONES RECORDS, VIRGIN RECORDS AND THE ROYAL SHAKESPEARE
COMPANY. HE STUDIED FOR A MASTER OF ARTS DEGREE IN COMMUNICATION
DESIGN AT MANCHESTER BEFORE BECOMING HEAD OF THE DEPARTMENT OF
GRAPHIC ARTS AT LIVERPOOL ART SCHOOL.
MIKE WILLIAMS WAS BORN IN HOBART, TASMANIA. AFTER MOVING TO BRITAIN HE
STUDIED INFORMATION SYSTEMS AT MANCHESTER UNIVERSITY THEN SPENT FIVE
YEARS CREATING INTERACTIVE INSTALLATIONS FOR MUSEUMS AND CORPORATE
CLIENTS. IN 1993, HE ATTENDED THE ROYAL COLLEGE OF ART IN LONDON SPECIALIZ-
ING IN INTERACTIVE MULTIMEDIA BEFORE JOINING NEVILLE BRODY AT RESEARCH
STUDIOS IN 1994. IN 1998 HE WORKED ON GRAPHICS FOR THE WARNER BROTHERS
FILM *THE AVENGERS* AND THE CD-ROM "FOREST OF SIGNS" WITH DAVID CROW.

148-149 FARROW DESIGN

CD AND PROMOTIONAL MATERIAL FOR THE BAND **SPIRITUALIZED**
WHICH DRAWS ON PHARMACEUTICAL PROCESSES. THE FACTORY WORK-
ERS WORE MASKS AS THEY ASSEMBLED THE CD PACKAGING.
OBSESSIONS COLOUR, SPACE, IMAGE, TEXTURE AND COMPOSITION.
MEANS ABILITY. **MATERIALS** CHOICE. **AUDIENCE** SELECT.
FARROW DESIGN, BASED IN CLERKENWELL, LONDON, CONSISTS OF FOUR DESIGNERS.
THEIR CLIENT BASE WITHIN THE RESTAURANT, MUSIC AND MEDIA INDUSTRIES,
INCLUDES ALL OUTPUT FOR THE DECONSTRUCTION LABEL, WITH ARTISTS SUCH AS
KYLIE MINOGUE, M PEOPLE AND THE CREAM ALBUMS. OTHER CLIENTS INCLUDE THE
PET SHOP BOYS, WITH RESPONSIBILITY FOR ALL GRAPHICS FROM RECORDS TO TOUR
MERCHANDISE AND VIDEOS. FARROW DESIGN HAVE WON SIX D&AD SILVER PENCILS
AS WELL AS AWARDS FOR BOOK DESIGN AND CORPORATE IDENTITY.

150-151 FUEL

TWO STILLS FROM AN ANIMATED TYPOGRAPHIC FILM ABOUT POSITIVE THINKING.
OBSESSIONS OUR MOTIVATION IS OUR OBSESSION. **MEANS** MEANS
EVOLVE AS WE CONTINUE TO WORK TOGETHER. **MATERIALS** WE CHOOSE
MATERIALS TO REFLECT THE REQUIREMENTS OF OUR IDEAS. **AUDIENCE** WE
DO NOT PRODUCE WORK WITH A SPECIFIC AUDIENCE IN MIND.
PETER MILES, DAMON MURRAY AND STEPHEN SORRELL FORMED FUEL AT THE
ROYAL COLLEGE OF ART IN 1991. AS WELL AS PRODUCING THEIR OWN MAGAZINES,
BOOK AND FILMS THEY HAVE WORKED ON MANY HIGH-PROFILE COMMISSIONS.
THEY ARE BASED IN SPITALFIELDS, LONDON.

152-153 NICK HIGGINS

A CLOUDBURST OF MATERIAL POSSESSIONS. CHRISTMAS CARD
UPDATING A LEONARDO DA VINCI DRAWING. WRITTEN BACKWARDS ON
THE CARD IS: "OH HUMAN MISERY, HOW MANY THINGS YOU SERVE FOR
MONEY?" THE ORIGINAL WAS CREATED WITH BIRO AND TRACING PAPER,
WHILE LATER VERSIONS WERE PRINTED. **OBSESSIONS** MY OBSES-
SIONS ARE A BIT UNDISCRIMINATING; I WOULDN'T LOOK AT ANYTHING
THAT DIDN'T DESERVE IT. **MEANS** MAKING PICTURES IS A WAY OF
BECOMING PERSONALLY INVOLVED; PICKING SOMETHING UP AND TURN-
ING IT OVER; OR HOLDING UP AND WAVING IT; OR HITTING IT WITH A
STICK. MAKING THINGS SUBJECTIVE. **MATERIALS/NONMATERIALS**
DEPENDS ON THE SUBJECT ENTIRELY, BUT MATERIALS ARE USUALLY SIM-
PLE AND CHEAP. AS LITTLE PROCESS AS POSSIBLE BETWEEN ME AND IT.
AUDIENCE ANYONE WHOSE EAR I CAN BEND OR EYE I CAN CATCH. OR
SLAP-HAPPY ART DIRECTORS.
NICK HIGGINS WAS BORN IN DEVON, ENGLAND IN 1960. HE STUDIED GRAPHIC
DESIGN [ILLUSTRATION] AT CENTRAL SAINT MARTIN'S AND HAS LIVED AND WORKED
IN LONDON AND NEW YORK AS AN ILLUSTRATOR. DESIGNING BOOK JACKETS FOR
HEINEMANN, HARPER COLLINS, VIKING PENGUIN AND PICADOR. HE HAS PRODUCED
ILLUSTRATION FOR *THE OBSERVER, THE INDEPENDENT, NEW YORK TIMES BOOK
REVIEW, THE NEW YORKER* AND *SELF MAGAZINE*. ANIMATED ILLUSTRATIONS FOR
THE BBC AND PRINT MATERIAL FOR THE ROYAL SHAKESPEARE COMPANY ARE SLOT-
TED IN BETWEEN SCULPTURE, PAINTING AND SELF-PUBLISHED WORKS.

154 ME COMPANY

DETAIL FROM AN ADVERTISEMENT FOR MENSWEAR LABEL **FIRETRAP**. THE
CAMPAIGN FEATURES FIVE COMPUTER-GENERATED DOGS WHICH ARE MEM-
BERS OF A GANG. THIS PROJECT WILL EVENTUALLY LEAD TO ANIMATED VER-
SIONS OF THE CHARACTERS. THE CHARACTER SHOWN IS THE MINDLESSLY
VIOLENT POT-NOODLE-EATING CLINT. **OBSESSIONS** THE JERRY SPRINGER
SHOW. **MEANS** INTELLIGENT CLIENTS. **MATERIALS/NONMATERIALS**
APPLIED MATHEMATICS. **AUDIENCE** CULTURALLY SENSITIVE 18-35 YEAR
OLDS WITH A HIGH DISPOSABLE INCOME.
ME COMPANY WAS FOUNDED IN 1986 BY PAUL WHITE. THERE ARE EIGHT PERMA-
NENT STAFF IN THEIR LONDON STUDIO. THE COMPANY INITIALLY TAILORED THEIR
WORK TO THE DEMANDS OF THE MUSIC INDUSTRY, TEAMING UP WITH A NUMBER
OF WELL-KNOWN ARTISTS, INCLUDING BJÖRK [A LONG-TIME CLIENT]. THEY NOW
ALSO EMBRACE ADVERTISING, TELEVISION GRAPHICS, FILM AND VIDEO IN THEIR
PORTFOLIO, AND THERE ARE PLANS TO MOVE INTO PRODUCT AND INTERIOR
DESIGN. ME COMPANY'S CLIENT LIST INCLUDES NIKE, DIET COKE AND MERCEDES.

156-157 UNITED STATES

158-159 BRIGID CABRY

BRAINCOOKIE. PHOTOGRAPHED AT THE OAKLAND COUNTY MORGUE. "I
ASKED THE PATHOLOGIST HIS FEELINGS ON DUALITY – THE MIND AS A SEP-
ARATE ENTITY FROM THE ORGAN OF THE BRAIN – AND THE ARTIFICIAL
RECREATION OF THE HUMAN MIND. HE SPOKE EMPHATICALLY AGAINST
ARTIFICIALITY AS HE SLICED THE BRAIN AS THOUGH HE WAS PREPARING
HIS DINNER". **OBSESSIONS** SIMULATIONS, DECEPTIONS AND COPIES.
MEANS IMAGES ARE CAPTURED DURING ON-SITE INTERVIEWS, WHETHER
TALKING TO IDENTICAL TRIPLETS ABOUT THEIR BOYFRIENDS OR DIS-
CUSSING ARTIFICIAL INTELLIGENCE WITH A PATHOLOGIST DURING A BRAIN
SLICING. **MATERIALS/NONMATERIALS** LIGHT, REFLECTION, TYPOGRAPHY,
PHOTOGRAPHY AND PROJECTION. **AUDIENCE** YOU.
BORN IN 1971 IN PHILADELPHIA, PENNSYLVANIA, BRIGID CABRY GRADUATED FROM
AMERICAN UNIVERSITY IN 1994 WITH A BACHELOR'S DEGREE IN GRAPHIC DESIGN.
SHE RECEIVED HER MASTER OF FINE ARTS IN GRAPHIC DESIGN FROM CRANBROOK
ACADEMY OF ART.

160 MATTHEW MULDER

BARK LITTLE DOGGIE. IN THIS POSTER, VIEWERS ARE FORCED INTO A
SUBMISSIVE PERSPECTIVE "I AM CHALLENGING THE VIEWER TO CONSIDER
WHETHER THEY ARE THE MASTER OR MASTERED WITHIN THEIR DOMAIN".
OBSESSIONS DISCOVERY. **MEANS** MY CURRENT DESIRE TO HAVE A
POINT COMES FROM THE PAST TWO-AND-A-HALF YEARS AT CRANBROOK,
GROWING UP WITH A BLUE-COLLAR MENTALITY, A SEARCH FOR UNDER-
STANDING, NOT TRUISMS, AND A PENCIL. **MATERIALS/NONMATERIALS**
THE MOMENTS THAT SURROUND US, WORDS, EPHEMERA, AND THINGS
THAT MAKE MARKS. MATERIALS I AVOID ARE QUOTES, "HOW-TO" BOOKS
AND IDEAS THAT COME FROM MARKETING WONKS. **AUDIENCE** ANYONE
I CAN GET TO LISTEN AND/OR SEE.
MATTHEW MULDER WAS BORN IN FORT WALTON BEACH, FLORIDA IN 1970. HE GRAD-
UATED FROM THE UNIVERSITY OF FLORIDA IN 1993 WITH A BACHELOR'S DEGREE IN
GRAPHIC DESIGN. HE WENT ON TO A NIGHT SHIFT JOB AT A WEEKLY COUPON MAG-
AZINE WHERE HE LEARNED 557 UNIQUE WAYS TO MAKE A STARBURST WITH THE
WORD "SALE!" WRITTEN IN THE CENTRE. HE COMPLETED HIS MASTER OF FINE ARTS
DEGREE IN 2D DESIGN AT CRANBROOK ACADEMY OF ART IN 1998, WITH THE DESIRE
TO INFORM AND CORRUPT AS WIDE AN AUDIENCE AS POSSIBLE WHILE MAINTAIN-
ING A RELEVANT VIEWPOINT.

161 DANIELLE FOUSHEE

BREATHING. STILL FROM VIDEO WHERE THE ARTIST IS TAKING IN HUGE
LUNGFULS OF AIR AND HOLDING THEM IN FOR AS LONG AS POSSIBLE.
OBSESSIONS I'M INTERESTED IN WHAT HAPPENS TO THE PHYSICAL
BODY IN CYBERSPACE; THE IDEA OF DISEMBODIMENT THROUGH THE
METAPHOR OF ILLNESS. **MEANS** INTELLECTUAL STIMULATION I GET
FROM MY CLASSMATES, READING, LECTURES, WRITING [A LOT], PARTICI-
PATION IN ON-LINE DISCUSSION FORUMS. **MATERIALS/NONMATERIALS**
I USE A COMBINATION OF VIDEO, STILL PHOTOGRAPHY AND PERFOR-
MANCE, IMPLYING MULTIPLICITY NOT ONLY THROUGH MULTIPLE IMAGES,
BUT THROUGH MULTIPLE MEDIA. **AUDIENCE** SMALL AUDIENCES.
DANIELLE FOUSHEE WAS BORN IN RALEIGH, NORTH CAROLINA IN 1974. SHE WAS
AWARDED A BACHELOR OF ENVIRONMENTAL DESIGN/GRAPHIC DESIGN BY NORTH
CAROLINA STATE UNIVERSITY IN 1996 AND RECEIVED HER MASTER OF FINE ARTS
DEGREE AT CRANBROOK ACADEMY OF ART IN 1998.

162-163 Warren CORBITT

[WH]Y DOES IT FEEL SO GOOD. EXPLORES THE SUPPOSED BOUNDARY BETWEEN VIEWED AND VIEWER. THE SAFE SPACE OF THE VOYEUR IS INVADED BY CHILDHOOD RELICS SEEN IN A PERVERSE, FETISHISTIC LIGHT. WHO IS BEING WATCHED? AND FROM BEHIND WHICH BLIND[ER]S? OBSESSIONS CONNECTING THE DOTS BETWEEN THE LINES [WITH SPRAY PAINT]. MY WORK EVOLVES IN A SPACE THAT I WISH TO FLIP ON ITS SIDE LIKE A TOP SPUN ON THE CEILING. IF YOU WISH, ADD SOME MIRRORS AND CALL IT A DISCO BALL. MEANS VIDEO PROJECTION, 35MM CAMERAS, ANYTHING ELSE I CAN THROW INTO THE MIX WITHOUT IT BECOMING HARD. MATERIALS/NEMATERIALS ANTIQUE TOYS, INVERTED TYPOGRAPHIC SPACES. AUDIENCE THOSE WHO WISH TO REVEL IN THE SPACE BETWEEN THE CORPORAL AND THE OPTIC.
WARREN CORBITT WAS BORN IN WILMINGTON, NORTH CAROLINA IN 1970. HE RECEIVED A DEGREE IN POLITICAL THEORY FROM VASSAR COLLEGE AND IS CURRENTLY A POSTGRADUATE STUDENT AT CRANBROOK ACADEMY OF ART. CORBITT WAS FOUNDING ART DIRECTOR OF *SWOON*, A WEB-BASED MAGAZINE FROM CONDÉ NAST. HE HAS ALSO WORKED FOR MAGAZINES SUCH AS *GO* AND *HOUSE & GARDEN*. FREELANCE CLIENTS HAVE INCLUDED *ESQUIRE* MAGAZINE, PRESCRIPTIVES AND VARIOUS WEB AND DESIGN AND ADVERTISING FIRMS.

164-165 Neil M. DENARI

INTERRUPTED PROJECTIONS, A BOOK EXPLORING THE CONTEMPORARY LANDSCAPE OF ADVERTISING, MEDIA SATURATION AND THE POETICS OF TECHNOLOGY IN OUR TIME. LAYOUT BY MICHIHARU SHIMODA OF SILENCE FOUNDATION DESIGN. ART DIRECTION BY DENARI, SHIMODA AND MASAAKI OKA IN TOKYO. OBSESSIONS AIRPORTS, PRECISION, *THE SYSTEM OF OBJECTS* BY JEAN BAUDRILLARD, THE FIRST FIVE MINUTES OF *BULLITT*, THE INFINITE LOS ANGELES, STATISTICS, THE MUSIC OF GLENN BRANCA, THERE ARE MORE ... MEANS FAST COMPUTERS RUNNING SOFTIMAGE MODELLING SOFTWARE; AND A SMALL, MOBILE, INTELLIGENT STAFF. MATERIALS/NEMATERIALS THERE ARE TWO REGIMES OF MATERIALS; ONE TO VISUALIZE WITH AND ONE TO BUILD WITH. FOR VISUALIZING I USE SMALL NOTEBOOK DRAWINGS, WHICH RECORD IDEAS WHICH ARE DIRECTLY EXPLORED ON THE COMPUTER. I DO NOT MAKE ANY PHYSICAL MODELS. AUDIENCE *INTERRUPTED PROJECTIONS* COMMUNICATES MOST READILY WITH OTHER ARCHITECTS, BUT GRAPHIC DESIGNERS IN THE STATES KNOW OF MY RELATION TO MEDIA AND ARCHITECTURE, SO THEY TOO HAVE BECOME AN AUDIENCE FOR THE ARCHITECTURAL IDEAS.
NEIL M. DENARI STUDIED ARCHITECTURE AT THE UNIVERSITY OF HOUSTON. IN 1982 HE RECEIVED A MASTER OF ARCHITECTURE FROM HARVARD UNIVERSITY AND THEN MOVED TO NEW YORK WHERE HE WORKED AT JAMES STEWART POLSHEK & PARTNERS AS A SENIOR DESIGNER. DENARI MOVED TO LOS ANGELES IN 1988 AND BEGAN WORKING AT COR-TEX, AND TEACHING AT THE SOUTHERN CALIFORNIA INSTITUTE OF ARCHITECTURE [SCI-ARC] WHERE HE IS DIRECTOR. *INTERRUPTED PROJECTIONS*, HIS FIRST BOOK, IS A GRAPHIC TWO-DIMENSIONAL PRESENTATION OF A SMALL EXPERIMENTAL SPACE CONSTRUCTED AT GALLERY MA IN TOKYO. DENARI IS WORKING ON HIS SECOND BOOK *GYROSCOPIC HORIZONS*. HE IS A VISITING PROFESSOR AT UNIVERSITIES IN THE USA, TOKYO, LONDON AND THE NETHERLANDS.

166 Brad BARTLETT

THE SPACE BEFORE THE EVENT. THE CHAIRS – HALF THEATRE SEAT AND HALF CHURCH PEW – ARE PART OF A VIDEO INSTALLATION REACTING TO A SPACE WITHIN THE MUSEUM THAT DIVIDES A GALLERY FROM A THEATRE. THE PROJECT IS AN ATTEMPT TO DISRUPT THE FLOW OF SPECTATORSHIP. OBSESSIONS THE SPACE DIVIDING/CONNECTING SCREENS AND FACES. MEANS STRONGLY INFLUENCED BY CHANCE AS A DRIVING FORCE TO INFLECT THE UNFOLDING OF EVENTS. MATERIALS/NEMATERIALS RANDOM DATA BURSTS, WAVES OF AM RADIO STATIC, DIGITAL VIDEO AND FEEDBACK LOOPS ON THE MASSMEDIASCAPE. AUDIENCE THOSE IN AND AROUND THE LABORATORY OF CRANBROOK.
BRAD BARTLETT WAS BORN IN RALEIGH, NORTH CAROLINA IN 1974. HE RECEIVED A DEGREE IN DESIGN FROM NORTH CAROLINA STATE UNIVERSITY, AND A MASTER OF FINE ARTS IN GRAPHIC DESIGN AT THE CRANBROOK ACADEMY OF ART IN 1998.

167 Peter HILL

HILL CONCENTRATES ON HOW WORDS AND LETTERS LOSE THEIR MEANING TO DYSLEXIA SUFFERERS, WHO BECOME OBSESSED AND DISTRACTED WITH FORM ITSELF. THIS IMAGE BEGAN AS LETTERFORMS, THEN TRANSFORMED INTO INCOMPREHENSIBLE GROUPS AND CLUSTERS. PETER HILL WAS BORN IN BOSTON, MASSACHUSETTS IN 1966. AFTER THREE YEARS AS AN ART DIRECTOR, A COURSE AT THE ART INSTITUTE OF CHICAGO REVEALED TO HILL THE "POTENTIAL AUTONOMY" OF GRAPHIC DESIGN. FROM 1995 TO 1996 HE WORKED AT THE KNITTING FACTORY IN NEW YORK AS A DESIGNER FOR THE CLUB'S PRINTED AND DIGITAL OUTPUT. HE IS A GRAPHIC DESIGN STUDENT AT CRANBROOK ACADEMY OF ART.

168 FUNNY GARBAGE

BODY VOYAGE. AN INTERACTIVE CD-ROM WHERE ONE CAN EXPLORE CROSS-SECTIONS OF THE INTERNAL ORGANS OF JOSEPH PAUL JERNIGAN, A DEATH ROW INMATE. AFTER HIS EXECUTION, JERNIGAN'S BODY WAS FROZEN AND SLICED INTO 1,871 PIECES, OFFERING A THREE- DIMENSIONAL VISUALIZATION OF FLESH, MUSCLE, BONES AND INTERNAL ORGANS. FUNNY GARBAGE DESIGNED THE INTERFACE FOR THE CD-ROM AND ALSO THE ACCOMPANYING BOOK. THE ARCHIVE OF IMAGES BELONGS TO THE NATIONAL INSTITUTE OF HEALTH. OBSESSIONS WORK, JAPANESE TOYS, LETTERFORMS, GARBAGE, GRAFFITI, BITING NAILS/SMOKING. MEANS PHOTOCOPYING, SILKSCREEN, CAMERA, COMPUTER, SKETCHBOOKS. MATERIALS/NEMATERIALS WHATEVER IS APPROPRIATE FOR THE JOB. EVERY PROJECT HAS ITS OWN NEEDS: SOMETIMES IT IS THE MAC, SOMETIMES IT IS PAPER, SOMETIMES IT IS FILM. AUDIENCE I DON'T KNOW, I HAVE A FEELING IT'S NOT FOR ME TO DECIDE [PETER GIRARDI ON BEHALF OF FUNNY GARBAGE].
FUNNY GARBAGE IS A DESIGN AND PRODUCTION COMPANY SPECIALIZING IN WEBSITE DESIGN, CD-ROMS, TITLE GRAPHICS AND PRINT CAMPAIGNS. CREATIVE DIRECTORS PETER GIRARDI AND CHRIS CAPUOZZO BEGAN THEIR ARTISTIC CAREERS PAINTING GRAFFITI ON NEW YORK SUBWAY CARS. THEY BOTH STUDIED AT THE SCHOOL OF VISUAL ARTS. GIRARDI BECAME CREATIVE DIRECTOR AT THE VOYAGER COMPANY, WHERE HE MET J.J. GIFFORD AND JOHN CARLIN OF THE RED HOT ORGANIZATION. FUNNY GARBAGE WAS FOUNDED IN 1996. CLIENTS INCLUDE THE CARTOON NETWORK, COMPAQ COMPUTERS, THE AMERICAN MUSEUM OF MOVING IMAGE AND NIKE.

169 Steve MURAKISHI

SMART CAR. THIS IS A CAR WINDSCREEN WITH SCREEN-PRINTED STICKERS ADHERED TO THE GLASS. IT IS PART OF A THEME ABOUT IDENTIFYING POLITICS; HERE THE ARTIST EXAMINES THE CAR AS AN ANONYMOUS BOX PEOPLE DRIVE AROUND IN, WHICH IDENTIFIES THE DRIVER VIA STICKERS THAT CARRY SLOGANS SUCH AS: CAUTION ASIAN DRIVERS; HAVE AN ENIGMATIC DAY; KIDDIE CARE; FEAR XENOPHOBIA AND BUDDHA PARKING PERMIT. OTHERS HAVE ID AND BAR-CODE INFORMATION. WITHIN THIS ENVIRONMENT THE ARTIST BELIEVES THE DRIVER ALSO BECOMES SOMETHING OF A FRAMED PORTRAIT. OBSESSIONS TOTAL AMAZEMENT ABOUT THE PLANET, WHAT MAKES CULTURE, MAKING AND THINKING ABOUT IDEAS, HAIR AND GOLF. MEANS PRACTICALLY SPEAKING I'M SELF-FUNDED. I TEACH TO WORK WITH YOUNG ARTISTS, SEEK GRANTS AND ALTERNATIVE FUNDING TO DO A RANGE OF COMMUNITY-BASED WORKS, AND THINGS OF A MORE SOCIAL NATURE. MATERIALS/NEMATERIALS I CHOOSE MATERIALS THAT REFLECT THE IDENTITY OF SOMEONE OR SOMETHING OTHER THAN AN ARTIST. I LOOK FOR "LOW-END" MATERIALS THAT DO NOT HAVE ART KEYED INTO THEM. I'D MUCH PREFER YOU TO RECOGNIZE ME AS A SCIENCE TEACHER OR A HAIRDRESSER. AUDIENCE MY PERCEPTION IS PEOPLE WHO MIGHT BORROW, SPECULATE OR REFLECT UPON THE IDEAS OF THE WORK. I TRY TO AMPLIFY A VOICE LESS HEARD.
STEVE MURAKISHI STUDIED SCULPTURE AT MICHIGAN STATE UNIVERSITY, BEFORE ATTENDING THE CENTRAL MICHIGAN UNIVERSITY WHERE HE SPECIALIZED IN PRINTMAKING. HE LECTURES AT UNIVERSITIES ACROSS THE USA AND HAS HAD WRITINGS PUBLISHED IN JOURNALS SUCH AS *THE NEW ART EXAMINER*. HE HAS BEEN AN INSTRUCTOR AT MICHIGAN STATE UNIVERSITY AND THE TOLEDO MUSEUM OF ART SCHOOL, AND IS HEAD OF THE PRINTMAKING DEPARTMENT AT CRANBROOK ACADEMY OF ART. HE HAS PARTICIPATED IN GROUP AND SOLO EXHIBITIONS, AND HIS WORK IS INCLUDED IN NUMEROUS PUBLIC COLLECTIONS.

172-173 Jeffery PLANSKER

"VERILY I SAY UNTO THEE, THESE STILTED PARCHMENTS ARE OF A WORK BODY ELEVEN YEARS HENCE, THUS KNOWN AS SUBVERTISING. THIS SUBVERTISING PONDERS AND THUS CHASTISES THE PERVASIVE AND TRIUMPHANT QUILT OF ADVERTISING IN ITS TOTALITY! MY DAILY WORK AS BOTH COBBLER, TANNER AND SHEPHERD OF SAID ACCELERATED SURPLUS ICONS AFFORDETH ME BOTH THE INSIDE UNDERSTANDING AND ENTITLEMENT FROM WHICH TO COMMENT UPON THIS MANIPULATION OF INNOCENTS/ 'TARGET AUDIENCE' VIA THE MOVING DAGUERREOTYPE THROUGH THE ORCHESTRATED 'CAMPAIGN' OR 'LAUNCH' OF AFTAFOREMENTIONED DISCIPLINES. THUS SAID, I RESPOND TO THE 'CLEAR-MINDEDNESS' AND 'SIMPLICITY' OF THE ADVERTISERS' VOICINGS [UNITED STATES] BY WALKING YONDER TO THE OTHER END OF THEE BURLEY PLANK. THUS THE WORK [SUBVERTISING] BECOMETH A DIRECT REACTION TO AN EXTREME. 'MEANINGFULLNETH' VS 'ABSURDISM'. THE PRESENT ADVERTISING/CONCEPTUAL REPRESENTATION OF ACCELERATED SURPLUS ICONS BEGS LASHINGS, NAY, WAISTBAND BROW-BEATINGS OR OTHER SUCH DEPANTS-INGS. ONLY THROUGH OUR STEADFASTNESS AND ALERT PLUNDERINGS DO WE FIND OUR BALANCE IN THE SHADOW OF THE JACKANAPES AND GOLIATHS OF THE MASSIVE MEDIA! IN HONOR AND DETERMINATION: JEFFERY SCOTT PLANSKER AKA: HO BEAUREGARD: ECCÉ HOBBO. 4TH REGIMENT-NEW ORLEANS." OBSESSIONS TO DRINK

THE SWEET GRAPE AND FEEL THE DELICATE LACE UPON MY COUNTE-
NANCE. MEANS A COBBLER BY TRADE, BUT ARMED WITH SECOND SIGHT
AND A CAPACITY FOR LETTERS. MATERIAL/IMMATERIAL I AM LIM-
ITED TO MY HUMBLE WORKBENCH; SOME LEATHER, A BIT OF STRING, A
CROCK OF RABBIT SKIN GLUE. AUDIENCE MY LORDS AND LADIES.
JEFFERY PLANSKER SPENDS HIS TIME DIRECTING TELEVISION COMMERCIALS AND
MUSIC VIDEOS AT PROPAGANDA FILMS IN LOS ANGELES, NEW YORK AND LONDON.
CLIENTS INCLUDE NIKE, COCA-COLA, REEBOK, PRUDENTIAL AND CHRYSLER. MUSIC
VIDEOS INCLUDE 10,000 MANIACS, URGE OVERKILL, RADIOHEAD AND
SOUNDGARDEN. PLANSKER HAS A BACHELOR OF FINE ARTS DEGREE FROM TUFTS
UNIVERSITY AND THE SCHOOL OF THE MUSEUM OF FINE ARTS IN BOSTON. HE
ATTENDED THE CENTER FOR CREATIVE STUDIES IN DETROIT, MICHIGAN, AS WELL
AS THE ART INSTITUTE OF CHICAGO FOR GRADUATE FILM STUDIES. PLANSKER IS
ALSO INVOLVED IN PE&Q SUBVERTISING WITH FELLOW ARTISTS OWEN O'TOOLE
AND HOBEY ECHLIN. PE&Q IS AN ANTI-AGENCY INVOLVED IN CRITICISM AND SUB-
VERSIVE STRATEGIES AIMED AT ASSORTED MEDIA TARGETS. HE IS THE FOUNDER
OF SUPPLY+DEMAND, INVOLVING NEW MEDIA ARTIST P. SCOTT MAKELA AND
GRAPHIC DESIGNERS GEOFF MCFETRIDGE AND JAMES SPINDLER. PLANSKER
HOSTS TWO JAZZ RADIO PROGRAMMES IN THE LOS ANGELES AREA.

174-175 J. ABBOTT MILLER

2WICE, A BIANNUAL MAGAZINE OF VISUAL CULTURE. THE CORE INTER-
ESTS OF 2WICE ARE PHOTOGRAPHY, PERFORMANCE ART, DANCE, FASH-
ION AND DESIGN. FOCUSING ON THEMES [IN THIS INSTANCE, FEET] AND
NOT SPECIFIC DISCIPLINES, ENABLES ABBOTT MILLER TO EMBRACE A
DIVERSE RANGE OF ARTISTIC ISSUES. NOTEBOOK TO LINK, COLLECT,
REPRESENT, GATHER, COAX AND SEDUCE. MEANS AN ENLIGHTENED AND
MAGICAL PUBLISHER NAMED PATSY TARR. MATERIAL/IMMATERIAL
PAPER, INK AND GREAT PHOTOGRAPHERS AND WRITERS. AUDIENCE
PEOPLE INTERESTED IN PHOTOGRAPHY, DESIGN, ART, FASHION AND THE
BROAD INTERSECTION IDENTIFIED BY THE PHRASE "VISUAL CULTURE".
J. ABBOTT MILLER IS DIRECTOR OF THE DESIGN STUDIO DESIGN/WRITING/
RESEARCH. HIS EXHIBITIONS AND PUBLICATIONS INCLUDE "THE PROCESS OF
ELIMINATION: THE BATHROOM, THE KITCHEN, AND THE AESTHETICS OF WASTE" [IN
COLLABORATION WITH ELLEN LUPTON], AND EXHIBITION DESIGN FOR "GEOFFREY
BEENE UNBOUND". HIS STUDIO IS ENGAGED IN PROJECTS WITH THE GUGGENHEIM
MUSEUM, AND IS DEVELOPING A MAJOR EXHIBITION FOR ROLLING STONE
MAGAZINE. ABBOTT MILLER IS VICE-PRESIDENT OF THE AMERICAN CENTER FOR
DESIGN. IN 1993 HE WAS AWARDED THE FIRST ANNUAL CHRYSLER AWARD FOR
INNOVATION IN DESIGN WITH ELLEN LUPTON.

176 REVERB

IDENTITY DESIGN FOR LANDMARKS OF A NEW GENERATION, A GETTY
CONSERVATION INSTITUTE GRASSROOTS INITIATIVE THAT ENVISIONS AN
ACTIVE ROLE FOR PEOPLE IN PROTECTING INDIVIDUAL AND COLLECTIVE
LANDMARKS FROM BEING LOST OR HOMOGENIZED. AS PART OF THIS,
TEENAGERS AROUND THE WORLD ARE GIVEN CAMERAS AND ASKED TO
RECORD THE LANDMARKS IN THEIR OWN LIVES. NOTEBOOK
OMNIVOROUS CONSUMPTION OF NEW AND OLD IDEAS, ARTEFACTS AND
MEDIA. MORE SPECIFILHLLY, GOOD STORIES, WHETHER TOLD IN SOUNDS,
THINGS, WORDS, IMAGES OR FOODS. MEANS THE UNIQUE COMBINATION
OF INDIVIDUALS, CLIENTS WITH VISION, THE OPEN ENVIRONMENT OF THE
STUDIO, THE LACK OF TRADITIONAL BUSINESS ASSUMPTIONS, A DYNAM-
IC AND FLEXIBLE ORGANIZATIONAL ARCHITECTURE, METHODOLOGY THAT
ALLOWS EACH PROJECT ITS OWN ARC. MATERIAL/IMMATERIAL
LANGUAGE IS AN ESSENTIAL PART OF OUR PROCESS. SO IS EACH PER-
SON'S EXPERIENCES AND TASTES. WE WORK WITH HIGH- AND LOW-TECH
MATERIALS: DIGITAL EQUIPMENT; PENCILS, SCISSORS, CAMERAS AND
THE PHOTOCOPIER. AUDIENCE OUR CLIENTS ARE DIVERSE AND OFTEN
PROJECTS HAVE MULTIPLE AUDIENCES SUCH AS EMPLOYEES, SHARE-
HOLDERS AND CUSTOMERS.
SOMI KIM, LISA NUGENT AND SUSAN PARR ARE THE PRINCIPALS OF LOS ANGELES-
BASED COMPANY REVERB. ALONG WITH FOUR OTHER DESIGNERS THEY HAVE
BUILT A WORKSHOP THAT ADDRESSES THE IDENTITY CONCERNS OF CORPORA-
TIONS, IN PRINT, ON AIR AND ONLINE. CLIENTS INCLUDE NIKE, MTV, THE J. PAUL
GETTY TRUST AND NETSCAPE.

177 THIRST

COVER OF 1998 CATALOGUE FOR GARY FISHER MOUNTAIN BIKES.
NOTEBOOK THE "THREE Cs": COMMUNICATION, COMMENTARY, COL-
LABORATION. MEANS WE HAVE IDEAS AND WE THEN DO SOMETHING
WITH THOSE IDEAS. OFTEN THOSE IDEAS ARE IN SERVICE TO THE NEEDS
OF A CLIENT; SOMETIMES THOSE IDEAS ARE APPLIED TO OURSELVES,
WHICH TEND TO BE MORE IN THE LINE OF COMMENTARY, AND THE WORK
DONE FOR THE LIVING, BREATHING, PAYING CLIENTS FALLS INTO THE
COMMUNICATION CAMP. MATERIAL/IMMATERIAL ATOMS AND BITS.
AIN'T NOTHING LIKE A PIECE OF PRINTED WORK IN YOUR HANDS, OR
POSTED UP ON THE WALL. THAT BEING SAID, SCREEN-BASED PRESENTA-
TION IS OFTEN THE MOST APPROPRIATE FORUM FOR CERTAIN COM-

MUNICATIONS. OR CUSHIONS IN THE SHAPE OF LETTERS. OR LASER-
PRINTED FAX SHEETS... AUDIENCE ANYONE WHO IS INTRIGUED, ENTER-
TAINED, INVOLVED BY WHAT WE DO, WHETHER IT IS DONE IN SERVICE TO
OUR CLIENTS OR OURSELVES. ANYONE WHO HAS EVER COME ACROSS A
THIRST PIECE AND THOUGHT "OH, THAT'S RATHER INTERESTING".
THIRST WAS FOUNDED IN 1981 BY PRINCIPAL RICK VALICENTI. IT AVOIDS SPECIAL-
IZATION AND HAS A VARIED CLIENT LIST INCLUDING GILBERT PAPER, GARY
FISHER MOUNTAIN BIKES, LYRIC OPERA OF CHICAGO AND THE CHICAGO BOARD OF
TRADE. THIRST'S WORK HAS WON NUMEROUS AWARDS AND BEEN WIDELY PUB-
LISHED. IN 1993 VALICENTI FOUNDED THIRSTYPE TO PROVIDE AN ARENA OF TYPO-
GRAPHIC EXPRESSION FOR DESIGNERS.

178-179 LORRAINE WILD

ILLUSTRATION FOR A LECTURE ENTITLED THE MACRAME OF RESISTANCE.
WILD EXPLAINS: "IT ILLUSTRATES THE POINT THAT DESIGNERS HAVE
THEIR OWN CLICHÉD PREJUDICES AGAINST STYLE [WHICH THEY TEND TO
DENIGRATE IN FAVOUR OF 'TIMELESSNESS']. THIS DOES NOT ACKNOWL-
EDGE THE FACT THAT VISUAL EXPRESSIONS GO THROUGH A 'LIFE CYCLE':
FROM INITIAL FASCINATION TO PROLIFERATION, UNTIL THEIR ULTIMATE
DESIGN – AND EVENTUAL RESURRECTION AS KITSCH. TIMELESSNESS
WITHERS IN THE FACE OF THE 'LIFE CYCLE'". NOTEBOOK THE FUTURE
VERSUS THE "LIFE CYCLE"; PESSIMISM VERSUS OPTIMISM; DEEP FEELING
VERSUS OVER-INTELLECTUALIZATION; EMOTION VERSUS RIGOUR; HANDS
AND EYES VERSUS HEAD, TYPE, TYPE AND YET MORE TYPE; THE IDEAL
VERSUS THE REAL; AND WHAT'S FOR DINNER. MEANS [PER THE SUG-
GESTION OF AMANDA WASHBURN, MY ASSOCIATE] ULTIMATELY, THE
APPLIANCE THAT COUNTS THE MOST SEEMS TO BE THE REFRIGERATOR.
MATERIAL/IMMATERIAL LIBRARIES AND COLLECTIONS OF ALL
KINDS, BIG AND SMALL. AUDIENCE I DESIGN FOR AN AUDIENCE THAT
READS THE VISUAL, AND ALWAYS MY COLLEAGUES AND STUDENTS.
LORRAINE WILD IS A DESIGNER AND EDUCATOR IN LOS ANGELES. SHE RECEIVED
HER BACHELOR OF FINE ARTS FROM THE CRANBROOK ACADEMY OF ART AND A
MASTER OF FINE ARTS FROM YALE UNIVERSITY. SHE HAS TAUGHT AT THE
CALIFORNIA INSTITUTE OF THE ARTS SINCE 1985, AND ALSO SERVES AS A PROJECT
TUTOR AT THE JAN VAN EYCK AKADEMIE IN MAASTRICHT, THE NETHERLANDS. FROM
1991 TO 1996 WILD WAS A PARTNER IN THE FIRM REVERB. HER CURRENT PROJECTS
INCLUDE THE DESIGN OF EXHIBITION CATALOGUES FOR THE WHITNEY MUSEUM OF
AMERICAN ART AND THE J. PAUL GETTY TRUST. WILD HAS EARNED MANY AWARDS,
INCLUDING THE CHRYSLER AWARD FOR INNOVATION IN DESIGN IN 1995. WILD IS ON
THE NATIONAL BOARD OF THE AMERICAN INSTITUTE OF GRAPHIC ARTS.

180-181 DEEP VIEW IMAGE RECORDED BY THE HUBBLE TELESCOPE. IT
SHOWS THE WIDEST VIEW OF THE COSMOS EVER SEEN, AND SO IS THE
MOST CONTAINED IN ONE PHOTOGRAPH, ONE IMAGE [AS AT THE TIME OF
PRODUCTION]. THE ENORMOUS DISTANCES MEAN THE OBJECTS AND
EVENTS RECORDED IN THE IMAGE HAPPENED AT VARIOUS TIMES IN THE
DISTANT PAST. "IT'S JUST ABOUT LOOKING OUTWARD, LOOKING BACK...",
SAYS SCOTT MAKELA.

192 LABOUR AND DELIVERY.

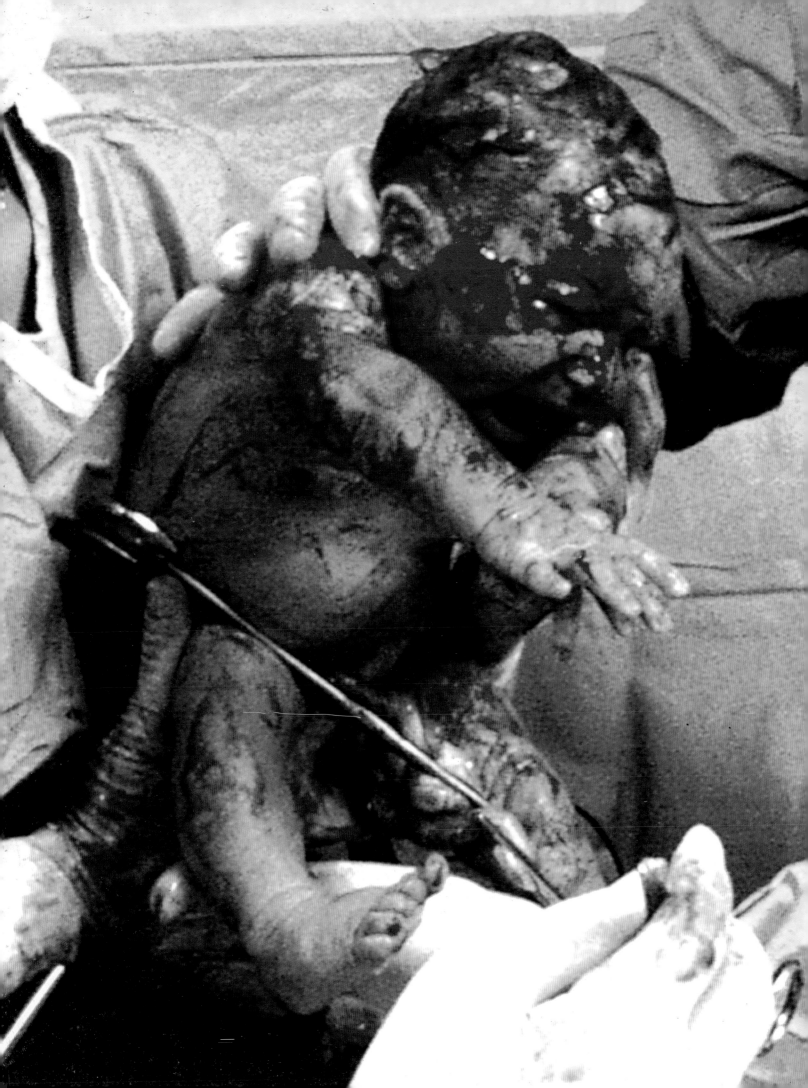